SERIAL
KILLERS

No. 41

S
A
To

Son of Sam was on way to kill again

'I wanted to go out in a blaze of glory'

By CARL J. PELLECK

The man police say is the Son of Sam was on his way to claim more victims when he walked into the arms of waiting detectives.

David Berkowitz, 24, had already written a letter—his third—addressed to Suffolk County and New York police and the press. He was going to leave it alongside his latest victim. It had no stamp on it.

In questioning after his arrest last night, Berkowitz said he hadn't quite made up his mind whether to stalk his next victims in Riverdale or in the Hamptons.

And he told police that he wanted to "go out in a blaze of glory" because he felt the cops were closing in on him. Sources said the letter made a similar claim.

'DID IT FOR SAM'

A pleasant-looking, slightly chubby young man, Berkowitz remained calm throughout the many hours of questioning at Police Headquarters.

He gave no reason why he started his killings in 1976 other than "I was anything . . . I

SERIAL KILLERS

FROM JACK THE RIPPER
TO THE ZODIAC KILLER

LIGHTNING
GUIDES

ISBN Print: 978-1-942411-33-8
eBook: 978-1-942411-34-5

Title Page Image: As many as 500 women and young
girls have disappeared in the last decade in the town
of Juarez, Mexico. Some are believed to be the victims
of the Juarez Predator, a serial killer whose identity
remains a mystery.

"I was born with the devil in me. I could not help the fact that I was a murderer, no more than the poet can help the inspiration to sing . . ."

—DR. H.H. HOLMES

We haven't always known how to talk about the murderers we now understand to be serial killers. Until the past few decades, we didn't even realize a separate classification was needed for these violent criminals.

The truth is that, for centuries, serial killers have been letting the sheer barbarity of their acts speak for them. Even if we had known how to name and talk about these predators, nothing we might have said about them—regardless of the moral or intellectual force of our pronouncements—would have given us the power to prevent their crimes.

Now that enough serial killers have been identified for us to be able to understand something about who they are, or were, what have we done with this information? We've made them into pop icons, superstar outlaws whose names or nicknames—Ted Bundy, Jeffrey Dahmer, John Wayne Gacy, Gary Ridgway, the Zodiac Killer, the Iceman, the Boston Strangler, the Hillside Strangler, the BTK Killer, Son of Sam—are as familiar as those of various celebrities.

In a word, serial killers leave us fascinated—and what a rich word that is. It's derived from the Latin root *fascinat-*, which means "bewitched" or "put under a spell." When we think about serial killers, there's a blend of fear and excitement, attraction and revulsion. It's the power of the predator to transfix the prey. It's why *The Silence of the Lambs* earned more than $130 million at the box office. It's what created a Sunday-night audience for eight seasons and 96 episodes of *Dexter*. It's what compelled you to pick up this book.

Perhaps the intense fascination serial killers arouse in us has to do with their assuming the role of society's bogeymen, how their primal acts of slaughter appease the hungry monsters under our beds. Thousands of serial killers have lived among us, and that's titillating in a terrifying way.

A harsh light directed at a few of the killers who roamed this precinct of human evil will illuminate their minds and methods, bear witness to their victims' terrible suffering, and offer the reader whatever measure of protection information can provide.

CONTENTS

first, a few facts

Pedro López was released from a mental hospital on a $50 bail in 1998; he was later convicted of murdering 110 young girls

TED BUNDY ONCE SAVED A DROWNING CHILD

CALIFORNIA HAS THE MOST SERIAL KILLER VICTIMS

You are 12 times more likely to be killed by a member of your family than by a serial killer

FBI officials suspect some 275 long-haul truckers of murdering more than 600 victims along US interstates

Are certain types of people more likely to be serial killers?

Despite the prevalent concept of serial killers as hyper-intelligent masterminds who exist on the extreme fringes of society, the reality is that most of them are surprisingly ordinary. The statistically typical serial killer is a white man of average intelligence. Forty percent of American serial killers have been black, while only 6 percent have been Hispanic, and less than 1 percent have been either Asian or Native American. Though all serial killers tend to strike first close to home (likely within the city or state where they live), women take it a step further, usually slaying either a family member or an acquaintance.

What method of murder do serial killers typically use?

Shooting is the most common way that serial killers take the lives of their victims, with 41.7 percent opting for a gun. Strangling happens in just less than 25 percent of cases, and stabbing occurs 15 percent of the time. Other recorded methods include drowning, overdosing on drugs, smothering, burning, and running over, but each of these happens in less than 1 percent of serial killer murders.

What country has the most serial killers?

The United States has not only seen the most serial killers since 1900, but the margin by which the US is number one is staggering. As of 2014, there had been 2,625 known serial killers in America. Next on the list comes England, with only 142.

Is serial murder common?

Serial killings account for no more than 1 percent of all murders committed in the United States. FBI crime statistics show there are approximately 15,000 murders annually, which means serial killers claim about 150 victims a year in the United States. The FBI also estimates that there are between 25 and 50 serial killers active throughout the United States at any given time.

Do women commit serial murder?

Indeed they do. Women serial killers have been found on every inhabited continent and in every country where serial murder has been recorded. Approximately 17 percent of all serial killings in the United States are committed by women. Since only 10 percent of all murders in the United States are committed by women, that means women actually commit a greater percentage of serial murders than other types of murder in the United States.

Are serial killers insane?

Legally speaking, no. To be classified as legally insane, a person must be unable to understand that what they are doing is against the law. Serial killers are more likely than the general population to exhibit antisocial personality disorders such as sociopathy, but these mental illnesses do not meet the criteria for legal insanity according to the American Psychiatric Association. Serial killers rarely are determined to be mentally incompetent to stand trial, and their lawyers seldom use an insanity defense, because the legal definition of insanity is so narrow.

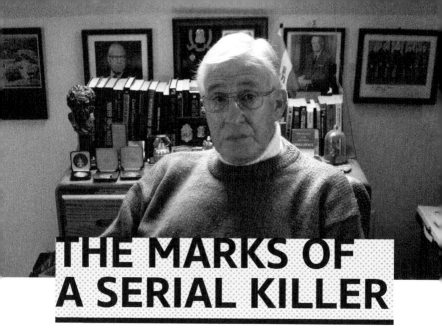

THE MARKS OF A SERIAL KILLER

WHAT EXACTLY IS SERIAL MURDER, AND WHO DOES IT?

The term *serial killer* is often credited to Robert Ressler, longtime FBI investigator and pioneer in the field of criminal profiling. British police and Los Angeles homicide detectives may have been the first to use the term, or a similar one, but it was Ressler who brought it into wide use in the 1970s as he urgently sought to name and understand a special kind of extremely dangerous murderer.

Above: Robert K. Ressler, a retired FBI criminologist, is considered America's leading serial killer expert. Ressler, pictured in his home office, started Forensic Behavioral Services International and consulted on the movies *Silence of the Lambs* and *Red Dragon*.

Ressler's sense of urgency was driven by the fact that, in the United States, the 1970s saw considerably more than twice the number of serial killings committed in the previous seven decades combined. And worse was yet to come—the number of US serial killings rose by another 33 percent in the 1980s, the decade that turned out to be the high-water mark.

Since then, for a number of reasons, serial killing has been on the decline in the United States. The first decade of the twenty-first century saw only half the number of serial murders committed in the 1980s.

In the decade between 1950 and 1960, researchers took the first steps toward distinguishing serial murder from both spree killing and mass murder, as they started to discern patterns in the motives and behavior of serial murderers—characteristics that could be said to set these killers apart from other practitioners of what was then called *multicide*.

Mass murder involves at least four victims who are fatally attacked by one or more persons during the same incident, usually at a single location. What the FBI once called spree killing involved at least two victims who were killed by the same

DID YOU KNOW

Dr. Henry Howard Holmes was among the first US murderers to be identified as a serial killer. Much of his story is told in Erik Larson's book, *The Devil in the White City*. Holmes may have killed as many as 200 people for the purpose of cashing in their insurance policies.

Richard Kuklinski, known as "The Iceman," enters the Bergen County Court where closing arguments are underway in his trial.

murderer or murderers in separate events that occurred at different times. For the FBI, the element that used to distinguish spree killing from serial killing was the serial killer's cooling-off period of at least one month between murders. Eventually, though, the concept of the cooling-off period was found to have no practical benefit for investigators, and so the FBI no longer makes any substantive distinction between spree killing and serial killing.

In 1998 the US Congress passed a law aimed at protecting children from sexual predators that included language about serial killing. The legislation defined serial killing as consisting of three or more murders with enough elements in common among them for an investigator to reasonably deduce that they had all been committed by the same person.

That legislative language was never meant to become the official definition of serial killing. It was intended as a guide for determining when it was appropriate to have the FBI get involved in helping local law enforcement agencies investigate a series of murders. But the term *serial killer*, as most people outside law enforcement use it, has come to reflect the language of that 1998 law.

Most people in the news and entertainment media, and members of the public, now use the term to refer to a lone killer who murders three or more victims, but not all at once. The killer's motives are understood to have something to do with psychological gratification, which frequently involves sexual contact with the victim, although the killer's motives for any one murder may include revenge, greed, and the search for attention, fame, or thrills, or any combination of the above. The victims are often murdered in a similar way, and they often share certain traits, such as age, race, gender, or general appearance.

The popular understanding of serial killers closely matches the profile the FBI used for several decades. But in 2005 the Bureau redefined some aspects of the term *serial killing*, and so the meaning of *serial killer* has changed in some ways.

Taken together, here is what these changes mean for the FBI's current definition of the term *serial killer*:

- The serial killer(s) may commit as few as two murders.
- The serial killer may have one or more partners.
- The serial killer(s) may commit the murders without a cooling-off period between the crimes.

Today's FBI defines serial killing quite simply: It is the murder of two or more victims, in separate events, by the same person or persons.

WHAT SERIAL KILLERS DO

SERIAL KILLERS HAVE DIFFERENT MOTIVATIONS AND PERSONAL PREFERENCES

The FBI now classifies serial killers in two broad ways—as characteristically organized or as characteristically disorganized. At different times and in different circumstances, however, an individual killer may fluctuate between these two classifications.

The organized serial killer is typically very methodical and maintains a high degree of control over the crime scene. This killer is act-focused and kills quickly. The organized serial killer often makes contact with a victim in one spot but commits the murder and disposes of the body in another. This type also tends to be better at covering up after the crime, often takes pride in the craft of killing, and may closely follow media coverage of the

murder. The organized serial killer usually has a higher IQ than the unorganized type, is more likely to be a respected member of the community, is or has been married or in a stable domestic partnership, and is often a parent.

The disorganized serial killer is far more impulsive, does little if any planning for a murder, tends to seize upon whatever weapon is at hand, and makes no attempt to hide the victim's remains. This murderer is process-focused, killing slowly and taking pleasure in the act. Other traits of the disorganized serial killer include a lower IQ than the organized type, a history of mental illness, an isolated social existence, and unemployment. Sexual violence and necrophiliac leanings are also common in this type of killer.

Apart from these two broad categories of serial killers—organized and disorganized—four subtypes have been identified by Ronald Holmes, a retired coroner and longtime professor of criminology at the University of Louisville. These four general

subtypes are based on what appear to be serial killers' typical primary motives, although a particular serial killer may also have secondary motives associated with a different subtype.

VISIONARY SERIAL KILLERS

Visionaries are usually psychotic. They are compelled to commit murder because, as this label implies, they have visions (and sometimes hear voices) that instruct them to kill. They often believe these instructions are coming from God or a demon, and some report that demonic possession is actually responsible for their crimes. David Berkowitz—better known as Son of Sam, the name of his homicidal alter ego—claimed that his orders to kill came from the devil and were channeled through a neighbor's dog.

MISSION-ORIENTED SERIAL KILLERS

Serial killers who are mission-oriented target individuals from specific groups that are deemed unworthy of human life— groups without which the world would be a better place, in the judgment of these killers. The highest-profile killers with a missionary orientation have gone after prostitutes, homosexuals, Jews, and African Americans. The Zebra Killers, a group of four black men operating in San Francisco in the 1970s, put their own spin on that dynamic. By shooting, strangling, and decapitating white women and men, they sought to better the world one murder at a time. The four were convicted of 16 deaths and many more attempted murders.

Left: Texas deputies question Delores Ball, whose husband Joe Ball was under investigation for feeding people to alligators.

HEDONISTIC SERIAL KILLERS

Hedonists commit murder primarily for kicks, and may or may not become sexually aroused during the act. The most concise way to characterize this group of murderers is to say that they kill for fun or profit.

By definition, this group includes plenty of thrill killers. These murderers crave excitement, and nothing does the trick like inflicting pain and causing terror. They relish the joy of the hunt, but the kill itself is paramount. The thrill killer's victim is usually a stranger. This kind of murderer kills quickly, without prolonging the act any more than necessary, and there is often no sexual contact with the victim. Carl "Coral" Watts, the Sunday Morning Slasher, was responsible for at least 22 and possibly more than 100 murders, mainly of young women, whom he killed in many different ways. One survivor reported that Watts had been extremely excited and clearly took enormous pleasure in the assault.

Lust killers like Ted Bundy also fall into this category, although Bundy had a very solid power orientation as well. Another lust killer was Kenneth Bianchi, who, along with his cousin Angelo Buono, committed the Los Angeles murders attributed to the Hillside Strangler. Lust killers derive sexual pleasure from torturing

William Lester Suff worked as a Riverside County, California, stock clerk. He kept largely to himself, although he enjoyed cooking his "special" chili for office picnics. Before Suff was revealed to be the Riverside Prostitute Killer, his job included delivering supplies to the governmental task force that was investigating the series of murders for which he was responsible. Suff has been on death row at San Quentin State Prison since 1995.

and even mutilating their victims. As they adapt to higher and higher levels of stimulation, they crave ever more excitement, and the time between their killings grows shorter and shorter.

Then there are the gain killers, typically driven by the desire for money and a comfortable way of life. This subset of hedonists includes the so-called black widow, often a poisoner who spoons death out in small doses to avoid attracting sudden unwanted attention. Dr. Henry Howard Holmes, who collected on his victims' insurance policies, was a gain killer, of the type known as a lethal caregiver.

When it comes to gain, a penny saved is a penny earned, which must have been the economic philosophy of Joe Ball, the Depression-era proprietor of the Sociable Inn along Highway 181 in Bexar County, Texas, an establishment known as much for the mysteriously high turnover among its staff of attractive waitresses as for its high-maintenance pit of well-fed alligators out back.

Contract killers fall into the group of gain killers, too—murderers like Richard Kuklinski, also known as the Iceman, who claimed to have carried out as many as 200 hits for crime families in New Jersey and New York over his 30-year career.

POWER-ORIENTED SERIAL KILLERS

Killers whose focus is power are not psychotic, although they are most likely to try for an insanity defense when they stand trial for their crimes. But they know the difference between right and wrong, and they're fully aware of what they are doing while committing their criminal acts, which usually involve considerable planning. Mental health professionals who evaluate these killers find them to be psychopathic, not psychotic.

WHAT DO SERIAL KILLERS LOOK LIKE?

Serial killers in the United States look like the population of the US, with many different racial and ethnic groups represented among them. Regardless of race or ethnicity, someone who is exposed and vulnerable to the conditions suspected of producing serial killers is as likely to go down that road— or not—as anyone

This kind of killer is obsessed with capturing a victim and compelling the victim's total obedience. A power-oriented serial killer will typically rape a victim, but these killers aren't driven by lust the way hedonistic killers are. For a power-oriented killer, sexual assault is primarily a means of domination and control. Angelo Buono, the other half of the Hillside Strangler killings, was a power-oriented serial killer.

This group includes angels of death, more often women, who surreptitiously murder helpless people who depend on them for medical or custodial care. Unlike the lethal caregiver who kills for financial gain, the angel of death kills to experience the feeling of ultimate control over life and death.

A power-oriented killer often falls into the *organized* category. A killer like this may quietly blend in—an apparently mild-mannered good citizen—or may stand out for personal qualities such as intelligence, charm, self-confidence, and the kind of charisma that wins deference from others and can lead to prominence in a local or professional community. Hervey Cleckley, a twentieth-century theorist of psychopathy, had a name for this kind of socially acceptable facade—he called it the *mask of sanity.*

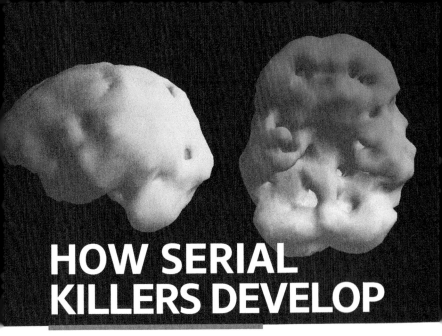

HOW SERIAL KILLERS DEVELOP

IS IT NURTURE MORE THAN NATURE?

J ohn M. MacDonald, an eminent psychiatrist of the early 1960s, outlined three traits in children and adolescents that he saw as predictors of violent behavior in adulthood: wetting the bed (enuresis) after the age of 12, starting fires, and torturing small animals. These three predictors are known as the *MacDonald Triad* (or sometimes the *triad of sociopathy* or the *homicidal triad*). MacDonald theorized that a young person who exhibited two of the three traits was at heightened risk of engaging later on in predatory behavior, possibly including serial murder.

Above: SPECT scan of the brain of murderer Kip Kinkel, a 15-year-old school shooter, who killed four people, including his parents, and wounded 25.

> **Paraphilia** Abnormal sexual desires, typically involving extreme or dangerous activities. Those associated with the behavior of serial killers include necrophilia (intercourse with corpses), fetishism (sexual fixation on specific objects), and partialism (sexual fantasies about certain body parts).

Other theorists, looking beyond the MacDonald Triad, consider its three predictors as signs of neglect in general, and specifically of physical, emotional, and sexual abuse. These types of neglect and abuse, they say, are the actual predictors of future violent behavior, especially when a young person's parents are separated, divorced, incapacitated by substance abuse, or impaired by any combination of these circumstances. Additional predisposing factors for the child may include being bullied and socially isolated. All these types of neglect, abuse, and cruelty may be instrumental in the development of the worrisome behaviors associated with serial murder.

The scientific study of serial killing's roots has since gone well past classifying the various motives that drive killers' violent behavior. By 1999, even Ronald Holmes, the criminologist who originally laid out the four basic sets of motives for serial killing, was chafing at the limitations of such taxonomies and calling for greater intellectual rigor.

To that end, he and two coauthors published an article in the *Journal of Contemporary Criminal Justice* that described what they called "Fractured Identity Syndrome," which they defined as the condition produced by a specific event or series of events in the childhood or adolescence of a person who later becomes

rrison, an American forensic psychiatrist, obtained John
n at his autopsy. Gacy's brain remains a symbol of how
about the mind of a serial killer.

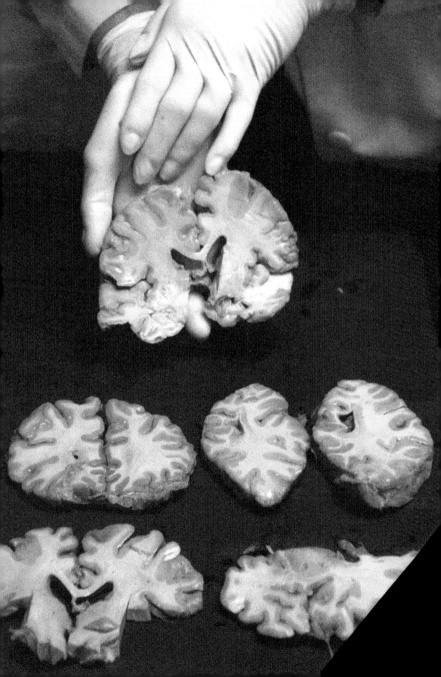

a murderer; such an event is a defining trauma whose impact fractures the developing personality. Holmes and his colleagues were quite deliberate in their use of the word *fractured*, with its connotations not of obvious, catastrophic shattering but of a small yet devastating crack, invisible to everyone except the person who has suffered the damage.

Another approach along the criminological spectrum—and a very influential one in terms of social policy, community-level interventions, and orientations toward mental health treatment of criminal offenders—is the approach of *social process theory*. From the standpoint of social process theory, anyone is susceptible to becoming a criminal in circumstances that encourage destructive relationships between the individual and the surrounding social processes and social institutions.

The absence of positive bonds with society and its institutions is what promotes criminal activity.

Social process theorists propose that criminals are people who have learned to engage in criminal activity, and that the path to a life of crime gradually opens out from family problems at home, learning problems at school, pressure from peers, and early, relatively minor scrapes with the law. Positive bonds with conventional society are what keep the majority of people from becoming the absence of positive bonds with society and is what promotes criminal activity.

Some researchers now hold out the hope that the key to serial killing will be discovered hiding in specific chromosomal abnormalities that have yet to be identified. So far, the few existing studies along these lines have been inconclusive, and this is an approach still very much in its infancy.

The critics of this approach also direct attention to the fact that a child who is abused, a child who is unable to escape from a situation he or she is powerless to control, will inevitably compensate for this weakness by systematically creating and escaping into an imaginary world. At that point, these critics suggest, as the fragile boundary between fantasy and objective reality is further weakened and finally lost to the child, the rich and enticing inner reality of dominance and control, a reality that has been taking on a more and more definite shape in the private, shadowy recesses of the mind, will begin to generate and intensify a relentless pressure on the psyche, until these compensatory, empowering fantasies finally demand to be acted out. And this, of course, has nothing to do with genetics.

THE UNKNOWN BRAIN

Dr. Helen Morrison, author of My Life Among the Serial Killers, *has studied more than 80 serial killers around the world. "The most frightening part about a serial killer is there is no reason," said Morrison. "We know that it is something in the electrical system that is acted on by hormor   the brain add   a*

A SERIAL KILLER BY ANY OTHER NAME

Usually concocted by newspaper headline writers, the nicknames given to serial killers range from vaguely grotesque to specifically literal. Here are the stories of some of the most memorable serial killer monikers.

DAVID BERKOWITZ
SON OF SAM
Between 1976 and 1977 New York City was gripped in terror as Berkowitz carried out a series of killings. He taunted the police, leaving notes at the scenes of his crimes signed "Son of Sam."

RICARDO LEYVA MUÑOZ RAMIREZ
NIGHT STALKER
Ramirez found the majority of his victims in the most unlikely of places—their homes. After breaking in late at night, Ramirez variously raped, shot, stabbed, and inflicted Satanic rituals on the 25 people he attacked, 13 of whom died.

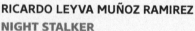

EDMUND KEMPER III
THE CO-ED KILLER

Despite his nickname, Kemper's victims weren't limited to the six college students he killed in the early 1970s—he'd also murdered his own grandparents at age 15, as well as his abusive, alcoholic mother.

TOMMY LYNN SELLS
THE COAST TO COAST KILLER

Sells's nickname proves to be quite literal: as a vagrant and carnival worker he roamed the country and claimed to have murdered more than 70 people. His execution in 2014 made headlines as questions arose about the testing methods of lethal injection drugs.

ANDREI ROMANOVICH CHIKATILO
THE BUTCHER OF ROSTOV

Also called "The Maniac" while he was on trial for his crimes, Ukraine-born Andrei Chikatilo was convicted of assaulting, killing, and defiling at least 52 people, though he claimed as many as 56 victims.

MURDER IN THE KEY OF D

JEFFREY DAHMER AND PAUL DUROUSSEAU

Sex is not the be-all and end-all of every murderer who kills for pleasure. For a hedonistic killer, the thrill of the hunt or even the possibility of material gain and other comforts can be at least as compelling a motive as the compulsion to dominate and violate another human being. But the fact remains that for some serial killers, murder is a primary means of sexual gratification.

GÖTTERDAHMERUNG

Among hedonistic killers, Jeffrey Lionel Dahmer (left) is one of the most infamous. He committed a series of gruesome murders over a 13-year period that began in 1978. Dahmer raped and dismembered many of his 17 known victims. His crimes included necrophilia and cannibalism.

{ **Götterdämmerung** Collapse or disintegration, marked by catastrophic violence and disorder. Literal translation from the German means 'twilight of the gods': Götter, plural of Gott (god) and Dämmerung (twilight). }

There was nothing overtly unusual about Dahmer's upbringing. Born in suburban Milwaukee in 1960 to a chemist father and a neurotic, somewhat self-obsessed mother, Dahmer was remembered as quiet and withdrawn in junior high school.

His family moved to Ohio, and Dahmer developed an obsession with biking around the neighborhood to look for road kill and then dissecting the animal bodies he found—an eccentric hobby, to be sure, but one that might have been the sign of a future veterinarian or forensic pathologist (although the youngster did once place a dog's head on a stake).

By the time Dahmer was in high school he was a heavy drinker, all but completely isolated from his classmates. He was also beginning to recognize his homosexuality. His parents divorced, his mother moved out, and Dahmer graduated.

One summer night in 1978, Dahmer picked up a 19-year-old hitchhiker, got him drunk, bludgeoned and strangled him, and buried the victim's body. Later he retrieved and dismembered the remains. He used acid to dissolve the skin and organs, and crushed the bones before scattering them in open fields.

He enrolled at Ohio State University, but was drinking so much that he missed most of his classes and had to drop out. At his father's insistence, he enlisted in the US Army, but his alcoholism got him discharged after two years.

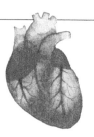

Unkind Cuts Jeffrey Dahmer, sometimes called the Milwaukee Cannibal, was not alone in having a taste for the kill. When Brazilian serial killer Pedro Rodrigues Filho murdered his father, he cut the old man's heart out and helped himself to a bite.

Closeup of police-padlocked door of apt. 213 at the Oxford Apartments after they found the remains of 11 men whom mass murderer Jeffrey Dahmer drugged, strangled, and dismembered while living there.

Dahmer spent some time in Miami before returning to his native Wisconsin in 1982. He looked for sexual partners in Milwaukee's gay bathhouses but found those encounters frustrating—he preferred to drug his partners so he could exercise complete control over them. Over the next few years, Dahmer was twice arrested for indecent exposure.

He killed for the second time in September 1987, then began luring more and more young men to their deaths. He later said he had been compelled by a fantasy of finding the perfect lover, one who would be not just beautiful but completely submissive. As he had done with the body of his first victim, he dismembered these victims' bodies, but now he also preserved their genitals in specimen jars. He tried to preserve their heads, too, but the acid he used destroyed their craniums. So he ate their flesh, hoping to make these young men part of himself forever.

In 1991 one of Dahmer's intended victims escaped and summoned police to Dahmer's apartment. Dahmer was convicted of 15 murders in Wisconsin and of the Ohio murder of his first victim. His sentence, handed down in 1992, amounted to nearly 1,000 years in prison. Dahmer was bludgeoned to death by another inmate in 1994 at the Columbia Correctional Institution in Portage, Wisconsin.

DUROUSSEAU'S DANSE MACABRE

Another hedonistic killer, Paul Durousseau, confessed to raping and murdering seven young single African American women between 1997 and 2003.

Durousseau joined the US Army in 1992. He was stationed for several years in Germany and then transferred to Fort Benning,

CELLULOID SERIAL KILLERS

1931

Psycho Arguably Alfred Hitchcock's most chilling work. Serial killer Norman Bates later spawned several sequels and a television series.

1991

M The German film has been credited with creating two genres: the serial killer movie and the police procedural.

1960

The Silence of the Lambs The first horror movie to be named Best Picture at the Academy Awards. Anthony Hopkins won an Oscar for his depiction of the murderous cannibal Hannibal Lecter.

Georgia, in 1996. In March of the following year he was arrested and charged with the kidnapping and rape of a young woman, but was acquitted several months later.

No one suspected Durousseau. Less than a month after he was cleared of those charges, the body of a 26-year-old woman from Columbus, Georgia, turned up near Fort Benning. She had been raped and strangled.

Not long afterward, stolen property was found in Durousseau's possession. He was court-martialed and dishonorably discharged from the army at the beginning of 1999. Married since 1995, he moved with his wife to her hometown of Jacksonville, Florida, that year, and the couple eventually had two daughters.

In Florida, he struggled to find work and had trouble holding jobs. He and his wife often fought about money, sometimes with violence on Durousseau's part. Meanwhile, also in 1999,

American Psycho One of the first serial killer storylines to be adapted into a musical, which opened in London in 2013. Although the story is fictional, novelist Bret Easton Ellis based the films' killings on true events.

2002

2000

Se7en Brad Pitt and Morgan Freeman play detectives who are led on a chase by a serial killer enacting murders in the manner of the seven deadly sins: envy, gluttony, greed, lust, pride, sloth, and wrath.

Dahmer Starring Jeremy Renner (who reportedly remained single for years as a result of playing Dahmer), this horror biopic recreates Dahmer's actual crimes, but changes all victim names out of respect.

Durousseau raped and strangled the 24-year-old woman who became the first of his Jacksonville victims.

In 2001, the same year Durousseau served nearly two months in jail for domestic battery, he was arrested for rape. He was jailed for 30 days and released with two years' probation.

In December 2002 he raped and strangled an 18-year-old woman. In January 2003 he raped and strangled four more women, all between the ages of 17 and 20, two of who were pregnant. The last three were killed on or after January 9, the day Durousseau began working as a driver for Gator City Taxi. He was arrested after witnesses identified him as the cab driver who had been seen with the last two victims.

Durousseau was charged with murdering six women in Jacksonville. In June 2007 he was convicted of the 1999 killing and sentenced to die by lethal injection. To the outrage of the other victims' families, the remaining five murder charges against Durousseau were dropped, because prosecutors feared the impact those cases might have on Durousseau's conviction if it went to appeal.

After his conviction, DNA evidence linked Durousseau to the 1997 murder near Fort Benning, and he confessed to that crime as well. Since December 2007, Paul Durousseau has been on death row at the Union Correctional Institute in Raiford, Florida.

IN THE LINE OF DUTY

THE FEW, THE PROUD, THE HOMICIDAL

Academic criminologists Tammy Castle and Christopher Hensley, published a paper in 2002 on possible connections between military service and serial murder. They wanted to know whether military training had reinforced pre-existing murderous tendencies in men who later became serial killers. The researchers found no evidence for boot camp alone as an explanation for veterans' subsequent serial killings, but they concluded that the issue deserves further study. Here are a few serial killers who served in the military, and the time frame in which their murders took place.

Fred Eugene McManus
US Marines
killed 5 people, 1953

Richard Raymond Valenti
US Navy
killed 3 teenage girls, 1973–1974

Joseph G. Christopher
US Army
killed 12 people, 1980

Ronald Adrian Gary
US Army
killed 4 people, 1984–1988

John Eric Armstrong
US Navy, killed between 5
and 18 people, 1992–1999

Jorge Avila Torrez
US Marines
killed 3 people, 2005–2009

THE SERIAL KILLER AND HIS PLUS-ONE

WHEN TOGETHERNESS GOES TOO FAR

Inspiring numerous movies, books, and even songs, crime couples often draw twice the public fascination as single criminals. Bonnie and Clyde's exploits captured the American public during the Great Depression, and although they may be the most infamous crime duo, they are certainly not the last. Couple murderers are crazy in love, and drive each other's propensity to kill. Here are some portraits of serial killers who found their perfect partner in crime.

THE LONELY HEARTS KILLERS
RAYMOND FERNANDEZ AND MARTHA BECK
UNITED STATES (ILLINOIS, MICHIGAN, NEW YORK)
4 VICTIMS, 1948–1949

Raymond Fernandez and Martha Beck, known as the Lonely Hearts Killers, tapped a willing pool of female victims by answering the women's personal ads seeking romance and companionship. Beck pretended to be Fernandez's sister, a ploy that encouraged their victims to trust the pair. Ironically, Fernandez met his future partner in crime by responding to Beck's own "lonely hearts" ad.

The film *Karla* (2006) is based on Canada's most infamous serial killers, the couple sometimes referred to as the Ken and Barbie Killers. In the crime drama, actor Misha Collins portrays Paul Bernando and actress Laura Prepon plays Karla Homolka.

THE SCHOOLGIRL KILLER AND HIS LOVELY WIFE
PAUL BERNARDO AND KARLA HOMOLKA
CANADA (ONTARIO)
3 VICTIMS, 1990–1992

A few months before Karla Homolka, 20, married Paul Bernardo, her third husband, she reflected on how disappointed he had been to discover that she was not a virgin. To make it up to him, she stole some anesthesia from the veterinary clinic where she worked, and on Christmas Eve she drugged her 15-year-old sister unconscious so that she and Bernardo could take turns raping her and videotaping it. When the comatose girl aspirated her own

vomit and died, the death was ruled an accident. But there was nothing accidental about the couple's subsequent rape and murder of two more girls, one of whom was 14 and the other 15. Homolka testified against Bernardo, who was sentenced to life in prison without parole. Homolka got 12 years and was released in 2005.

THE SUNSET STRIP KILLERS
DOUGLAS CLARK AND CAROL MARY BUNDY
UNITED STATES (CALIFORNIA)
7 VICTIMS, 1980

Douglas Clark and Carol Mary Bundy met at a bar, where Bundy was stalking a married man who had ended his affair with her. It didn't take Clark and Bundy long to discover what they had in common—a grim fascination with sexual violence, which came to include not just the rape and murder of young prostitutes but also their decapitation, followed by Clark's necrophiliac enjoyment of the women's mutilated bodies or body parts. As for the object of Bundy's unrequited love, Bundy finally shot him dead, cut off his head, and enlisted Clark's help to dispose of it.

THE SEX-SLAVE KILLERS
GERALD AND CHARLENE GALLEGO
UNITED STATES (CALIFORNIA, NEVADA, OREGON)
10 VICTIMS, 1978–1980

Gerald and Charlene Gallego were a precision team. A typical operation had Charlene approaching a teenage girl or young woman and luring her to the couple's vehicle with the promise of a party or a job. Then Gerald would head for the Sierra Nevada Mountains, where he and Charlene both raped the girl. Afterward, Gerald would drive to a different spot, kill the girl, and bury or simply dump her body. Gerald was sentenced to death but died of cancer in prison before he could be executed. Charlene, in exchange for testifying against her husband, served 16 years and 8 months in a Nevada prison. She was released in 1997.

PREDATORS OF THE GREAT PLAINS
CHARLES STARKWEATHER AND CARIL ANN FUGATE
UNITED STATES (NEBRASKA, WYOMING)
7 VICTIMS, 1957–1958

Caril Ann Fugate met Charles Starkweather, 18, when she was a rebellious girl of 13 living in Lincoln, Nebraska. Starkweather killed Fugate's mother, stepfather, and two-year-old half-sister and stashed their bodies in the property's outhouse and chicken coop. Then he and Fugate embarked on a rampage that left seven people dead—a 70-year-old family friend of Starkweather's, a teenage couple, a wealthy industrialist along with his wife and their maid, and a traveling salesman.

Former fugitives Alton Coleman and Debra Brown confer prior to a brief court appearance in Cincinnati.

MIDWEST MARAUDERS
ALTON COLEMAN AND DEBRA DENISE BROWN
UNITED STATES (ILLINOIS, INDIANA, KENTUCKY, MICHIGAN, OHIO, WISCONSIN)
8 VICTIMS, 1984

Debra Denise Brown had no history of violence until she was 21, when she abandoned her fiancé and took up with Alton Coleman, 28, a habitual killer and rapist. Once under Coleman's spell, Brown joined him in a multistate orgy of armed robbery, kidnapping, rape, torture, and murder. Their victims included children and elderly people. The pair targeted African Americans like themselves, finding it relatively easy to move unchallenged through black neighborhoods. Coleman was executed by lethal injection in 2002. Brown's death sentence was commuted to life in prison without parole, in view of what came to be recognized as her borderline mental retardation, her dependent personality, and the likely influence of these psychological issues on her master-slave relationship with Coleman.

SENIOR MOMENTS TO REMEMBER
RAY AND FAYE COPELAND
UNITED STATES (MISSOURI)
5–12 VICTIMS, 1986–1989

The typical serial killer's career begins in young adulthood. But Ray and Faye Copeland delayed their debut until their golden years, when they killed at least five drifters and hobos employed as short-term hands on their cattle farm. Faye managed to stitch up a cozy winter quilt from the victims' clothing before she and her husband, in 1991, became the oldest couple ever sentenced to death in the United States. Two years later Ray Copeland died in prison of natural causes at the age of 78. In 1999, when Faye was 78, her death sentence was commuted to life imprisonment. After suffering a stroke, she was granted a medical parole and died 16 months later at the Morningside Center Nursing Home in Chillicothe, Missouri. She was 82.

"The Bloody Benders" John, his wife, son, and daughter, Kate, ran an inn in Labette County, Kansas. Between 1871 and 1873 they killed about a dozen travelers by crushing their skulls with a hammer and cutting their throats, subsequently stealing their belongings. When the crimes were discovered, the Benders fled and were never captured.

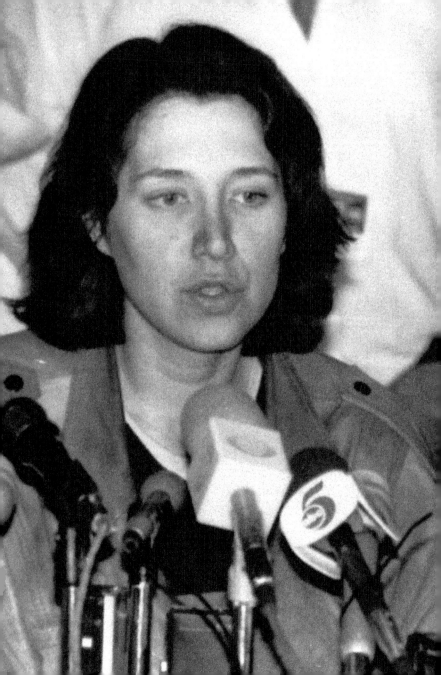

THE GODPARENTS OF MATAMOROS

ADOLFO DE JESÚS CONSTANZO
AND SARA MARÍA ALDRETE
MEXICO (TAMAULÍPAS)
16 VICTIMS, 1987–1989

Adolfo de Jesús Constanzo, born in Florida to a Cuban mother, and Sara Aldrete, a native of Mexico who became a US resident, were the padrino and padrina (godfather and godmother) of a religious cult based at Rancho Santa Elena, a compound in the desert outside Matamoros, a city in the Mexican state of Tamaulípas across the Rio Grande from Brownsville, Texas. The cult combined elements of Santería, Palo Mayombe (two religions with elements of black magic), and Mexican *brujería* (witchcraft), not to mention blood sacrifice. Constanzo raped and ritually killed an assortment of mostly male prostitutes, homeless people, and drug dealers. Aldrete boiled their body parts in a large ceremonial pot used for that purpose. When police were about to close in on Constanzo, he ordered himself shot to death by an assistant.

Left: Sara Aldrete, 24, companion of Adolfo de Jesús Constanzo, speaks with reporters after her arrest in Mexico City.

CON- STANZO'S CULT

Members of Adolfo de Jesús Constanzo's cult abducted Mark Kilroy, an American college student on spring break in Mexico, from outside a bar in Matamoros and took him to be ritually slain at Constanzo's desert compound. Several weeks later, a drug dealer inadvertently led Mexican authorities to the compound, where they found Kilroy's mutilated body among some 25 others.

THE SIGN OF DEATH

KNOWNS AND UNKNOWNS ABOUT THE ELUSIVE ZODIAC KILLER

WHAT WE KNOW . . .

The Zodiac Killer operated in Northern California between the late 1960s and early 1970s

There are seven confirmed victims, two of whom survived

The killer's name originated in a letter to the *San Francisco Examiner* that opens with the words, "This is the Zodiac speaking"

In his book, *The Most Dangerous Animal of All*, Gary Stewart claims his own biological father, Earl Van Best, Jr., was the Zodiac Killer

. . . AND WHAT WE DON'T

The killer's identity

The total number of people murdered by the Zodiac Killer (at least four more murders are suspected, and the killer claimed in written communications to have taken 37 lives)

Right: San Francisco homicide inspectors David Toschi, left, and William Armstrong go through a murder victim's clothes at the morgue in the Hall of Justice in San Francisco.

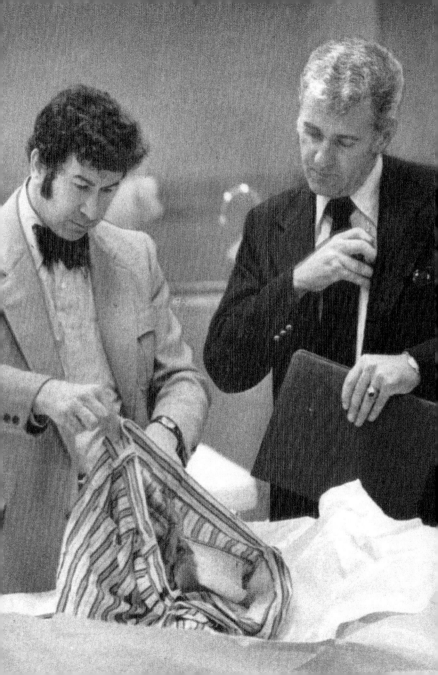

COLD CASE

1. MILES, WILLIE
12/20/79

Cold Case
1. Eige Sober Adler
Case # 87357

TO CATCH
A SERIAL
KILLER

SIX BEST PRACTICES FROM
THE FBI FOR MANAGING AN
INVESTIGATION

1 When a community becomes aware that a serial killer is at large, tension and fear dominate the public imagination. Police, homicide detectives, and prosecutors quickly come under pressure from victims' families, as well as from politicians and the media. In these circumstances, investigators' ability to gather and protect evidence and prosecute the crimes successfully will depend on the steady influence and authority of strong leaders up and down the law enforcement chain of command.

2 It's not uncommon for a serial killer to abduct a victim from one jurisdiction and commit the murder in another, or to dispose of a victim's body in a place other than where the killing occurred. These factors point to the need for a task force made up of representatives from the relevant agencies in the various jurisdictions.

3 To help investigators keep track of the many pieces of data that a series of murders necessarily entails, an automated case-management system is indispensable.

4 Even more than other types of homicides, a series of murders calls for an investigation that uses a team of crime analysts to create timelines, gather background information about suspects, and look for similarities between what may appear at first to be separate murders.

5 The investigation of a series of murders will benefit immensely from consistent forensic services. If different forensic evidence teams are sent to the different crime scenes, and if different crime labs process the evidence, then there must be clear and precise communication between the teams and the labs. In the ideal investigation, the same team is sent to every one of the crime scenes, and all the evidence from every crime scene is sent to a single crime lab.

6 Investigators need to develop a clear media plan, one that strikes a balance between informing the public and protecting the integrity of the investigation.

SLAYING SOLO

TWISTED SISTERS DOING IT FOR THEMSELVES

For about 50 to 70 percent of women who commit murder multiple times, serial killing is a one-person operation. The woman who fits this profile tends to be meticulous and purposeful.

Above: The serial killer Countess Elizabeth in the film *Daughters of Darkness* at the desolate seaside hotel where she claimed her victims.

Due to the fact that she is so calculating and organized, she is often able to kill undetected for much longer than her male counterparts or than women who kill in partnership with men. Another reason for her success at staying under the radar is the stereotype of the serial killer as a psychopathic white male. When a series of murders comes to light, people typically don't suspect the killer might be a woman. She also benefits from an upside of sexism—the assumption that a woman is innately too kind and caring to snuff out even a single human life, much less the lives of a whole unlucky procession.

This type of killer is most likely to murder people she already knows—her own or someone else's children, other family members, a string of husbands or partners, or adults in her care. She may kill for erotic gratification, for revenge, or to feel powerful and in control. Female serial killers tend to mix one or more of these motives with a desire for material gain. Here are some portraits from the female side of the serial killers' gallery.

COUNTESS ELIZABETH BÁTHORY
KINGDOM OF HUNGARY, 1560–1614
BEATING, BITING, FREEZING, STARVING, MUTILATION
80–650 VICTIMS, 1585–1610

Readers of a certain age and sensibility will recall the cult lesbian vampire movie *Daughters of Darkness*, starring Delphine Seyrig as a 1970s-era Countess Elizabeth Báthory. The film portrays the countess as mentor to a bevy of bi-curious acolytes who yield to dark pleasures by the flattering light of pink-shaded lamps.

But in late-sixteenth-century Hungary, the goings-on *chez* Báthory couldn't have been nearly so much fun. Folklore has it that the countess maintained a beauty regimen of bathing in her victims' blood, and that fresh victims-to-be were forced to lap up the gore from the countess's body.

The countess was arrested in 1610, having outraged her aristocratic peers by preying on their daughters after she tired of peasant girls. In the end, though, it was decided that a trial, to say nothing of an execution, would be politically destabilizing and unbelievably gauche. Countess Báthory spent the last four years of her life under house arrest, in solitary confinement and reportedly "bricked in."

BELLE SORENSON GUNNESS
UNITED STATES, 1859–1908
POISONING, BLUDGEONING
13–42 VICTIMS, 1880s–1908

Brynhild Paulsdatter Størseth, a native of Norway who stood six feet tall, emigrated to the United States at the age of 21 or 22. Her life from that point on was propelled by a curious mixture of good and bad luck.

As good luck would have it, Belle, as she now called herself, met an eligible Chicago businessman, Mads Sorenson, and two years later the happy couple opened a confectionery. But if the Sorensons were lucky in love, they were unlucky in business. To make matters worse, within a year their store mysteriously burned to the ground. Happily, the building was insured, and the couple collected on the loss. Meanwhile, the Sorensons had started a family. Sadly, two of their daughters died as infants.

Right: Suspected murderer Belle Gunness with her children Lucy Sorenson, Myrtle Sorenson, and Philip Gunness in 1904.

IGNOBLE SADIST

Muscovite noblewoman Darya Nikolajevna Saltykova died in 1801 after spending 33 years in solitary confinement. Between 1757 and 1764 she tortured and murdered more than 100 victims— three men and the rest women and little girls. Most were her serfs. Before she was sent to her prison cell, Russian Empress Catherine the Great put her on public display in Moscow for one hour.

But it happened that the children's lives, like the couple's store, were insured. Both death benefits were paid, and after a time all was well again. Until misfortune struck again—Mads Sorenson died, in very odd circumstances. Miraculously, not only did he have life insurance, but he died on the very day when his life happened to be insured by two overlapping policies. This time, too, the insurance company honored Belle's claim, and she used the proceeds to buy a farm on the outskirts of La Porte, Indiana.

Fortune smiled on Belle, and she connected with Peter Gunness, a widower. The two were married in La Porte. But only a week after their wedding, Peter's infant daughter died while alone in their house with Belle. And, tragically, a bizarre household accident took Peter's life only eight months later. Remarkably, however, his life was insured, and Belle was able to mourn her loss without the distraction of financial ruin.

Over the years that followed, Belle was lucky enough to attract and wed many lonely suitors and brighten their prudently insured lives. Before her death—said to have occurred in 1908, although discussion continues about whether the charred and decapitated remains found in Belle's smoldering house actually *were* Belle—this assiduous black widow amassed insurance payouts totaling $250,000, nearly $6 million in today's dollars. She is rumored to have laid some 40 unfortunates to rest on the property it was her good fortune to acquire.

ANNA MARIE HAHN
UNITED STATES, 1906–1938
POISONING
5 VICTIMS, 1932–1937

Anna Marie Hahn arrived in the United States from her native Germany when she was 21. As a live-in caregiver for elderly German men in Cincinnati, Ohio, she found innovative ways to plunder their resources. Her slow, patient methods, apart from poisoning, included piecemeal embezzlement and the kind of personal attention that could get her prominently mentioned in a future victim's will. Her crimes were finally investigated and exposed when police were alerted by suspicious auditors at her deceased benefactors' banks. Hahn became the first woman to be executed in Ohio's electric chair.

DOROTHEA PUENTE
UNITED STATES, 1929–2011
POISONING, DRUG OVERDOSING
9 VICTIMS, 1982–1988

As the proprietor of a boarding house in Sacramento, Dorothea Puente was more concierge than landlady. Not only did she make sure her elderly tenants take their medication, but she collected their mail, cashed their benefit checks, personally paid the named recipients a fraction of the checks' value, and kindly arranged for the old dears to be interred in her backyard right after they died of "natural causes," or possibly right before.

AILEEN WUORNOS

UNITED STATES, 1956–2002
SHOOTING
6 VICTIMS, 1989–1990

Even the briefest survey of women serial killers calls for a word about the formidable Aileen Wuornos. The image of Wuornos, a pistol-packing hitchhiker and highway robber, is the same as the image popular culture associates with male serial killers. That familiar archetype is why Wuornos is much better known than her less flamboyant sisters in crime.

Wuornos was the subject of the film *Monster,* and that just about sums it up— her dreadful childhood; her Borderline Personality Disorder; her string of arrests for petty crimes; her life of prostitution, briefly suspended when she married an elderly admirer, and quickly resumed after she whacked him with his cane and the union failed; her return to the streets, specifically Interstate 75 in Florida; and the series of fatal shootings that

DID YOU KNOW

Her chilling portrayal of Aileen Wuornos in *Monster* won Charlize Theron an Academy Award. Theron received her Oscar on February 29, 2004— which would have been Wuornos's 48th birthday.

HOW ALIKE ARE SERIAL KILLERS?

Aside from the obvious—the act of killing—women and men who commit serial murder don't have all that much in common. Of course, there are individual motivations and circumstances for each murder, but statistics show that people who fit the following profiles commit the majority of serial murders. From their motivations to their methods, here are a few ways in which men and women differ when it comes to serial killing.

MEN

KILL STRANGERS

TORTURE THEIR VICTIMS

ARE BLUE-COLLAR WORKERS

KILL FOR POWER OR THRILL

WHITE

ARE OR HAVE BEEN MARRIED

WOMEN

KILL PEOPLE THEY KNOW

POISON THEIR VICTIMS

ARE NURSES OR CAREGIVERS

KILL FOR MONEY

made this an apt title for the film. Wuornos and her attorney sold the rights to her story within two weeks of her arrest for killing the first of the six men she is known to have shot and robbed by using the pretext of flagging them down on the freeway to turn a trick.

Wuornos entered a plea of *nolo contendere* to charges of murdering her last five victims, and she was tried only for killing the first. In that case, as in the other five, she said she had killed in self-defense. The jury might have believed her, too, if her attorneys had run her first victim's name through the FBI database, where records showed that he had served 10 years for a brutal rape in another state.

Wuornos later retracted her claim of self-defense in the murders of her five other victims. "I killed those men in the first degree, robbed them and killed them, cold as ice," she told Nick Broomfield, a documentary filmmaker, shortly before her death by lethal injection. "And I'd do it again, too." But she never changed her story about the man who was her first known victim.

JOANNA DENNEHY
UNITED KINGDOM, B.1982
STABBING
3 VICTIMS, 2013

Over a 10-day period, in three separate murders, Joanna Dennehy, mother of two, fatally stabbed her landlord and two male housemates, one of whom imagined he was in love with her. She dumped their bodies in ditches outside the city of Peterborough, 75 miles north of London. Her landlord's body, discovered in a suggestive pose, was partially clothed in a black sequined dress. Dennehy's crimes became known as the Peterborough ditch murders.

Serial killer Joanna Dennehy who took a grinning selfie photograph of herself as she searched out further victims.

At her trial, Dennehy declined to explain her motives, and she stunned her lawyers by immediately confessing to the three murders. "I've pleaded guilty and that's that," she told the court. She followed that statement with a spontaneous confession to the attempted murder of two more men. Dennehy laughed as the judge called her a psychopathic serial killer and sentenced her to life in prison without possibility of parole.

OGRESS OF READING

One of the most prolific serial killers in Victorian England, British 'baby farmer' Amelia Dyer charged poor mothers £5 to take in illegitimate infants under the pretext of caring for them. She is thought to have murdered as many as 400 children, though she was tried and hanged for only one murder.

JUANA BARRAZA

MEXICO, B.1958
BLUDGEONING, STRANGLING
11–49 VICTIMS, 2002–2006

Juana Barraza, the Mexican serial murderer known as *La Mataviejitas* (The Little Old Lady Killer), never forgave her alcoholic mother for throwing her out of the house at the age of 12. Barraza's performances as an amateur wrestler known as *La Dama del Silencio* (The Lady of Silence) failed to quiet her rage, so she helped old ladies across the street and killed them. She would accompany the victim home, subdue her with a blow to the head, then strangle her with a telephone cord, a pair of tights, or the stethoscope she carried when posing as a nurse and pretending to offer free checkups to the dowagers she picked up on the streets. Barraza robbed her victims after killing them. In 2008 she began serving a prison sentence of 759 years.

Right: Juana Barraza was caught after she was seen leaving the scene of the murder of an 82-year-old woman. Barraza is suspected to have murdered at least 11 elderly women. She was arrested on suspicion of being the serial murderer known as the "little old lady killer," who preyed on elderly women and murdered them in their homes in Mexico City.

EVIDENCE AND EXPOSURE

Leaving no trail of blood or bodies in his tracks, John George Haigh likely thought he could get away with murder and enjoy his victims' fortunes, but time would tell otherwise.

JOHN GEORGE HAIGH
BORN: July 24, 1909
PLACE: Stamford, Lincolnshire, UK
NICKNAME: The Acid Bath Murderer

McSWANN AND HIS MOTHER

FIRST MURDER

METHOD: BLUDGEONING
DISPOSAL: DISSOLVED IN AN ACID BATH

" When I discovered there were easier ways of making a living than to work long hours in an office, I did not ask myself whether I was doing right or wrong . . . I merely said,

THIS IS WHAT I WISH TO DO. "

Sulphurous Acid

SECOND MURDER

VICTIM: FORMER EMPLOYER WILLIAM DONALD McSWAN
METHOD: BLUDGEONING OVER THE HEAD
DISPOSAL: DISSOLVED THE BODY USING SULFURIC ACID & DRAINED RESULTS INTO SEWERS

DR. ARCHIBALD HENDERSON AND ROSALIE HENDERSON

METHOD: SHOOTING
DISPOSAL: DISSOLVED THE BODIES IN OIL DRUMS FILLED WITH SULFURIC ACID

FINAL MURDER

THIRD MURDER

METHOD: SHOOTING
DISPOSAL: DISSOLVED IN AN ACID BATH

OLIVE DURAND-DEACON

HAIGH FORGED PAPERWORK TRANSFERRING ALL THE ASSETS OF HIS VICTIMS TO HIMSELF AND RETAINING THEIR PROPERTY

1934 ARESTED

GUILTY

AUGUST 10, 1949
HANGED

IN FLAGRANTE DELICTO

TIGHTENING THE NOOSE ON THE TURBAN KILLER

Throughout the 1960s and early 1970s, Abul Djabar raped and killed at least 65 boys and young men in Afghanistan's Kabul Province. His signature was strangulation with his turban.

The discovery of more and more violated male bodies put Kabul's authorities under intense pressure, and two innocent men were executed for Djabar's crimes. Then, in October 1970, police caught Djabar in the act.

Justice, deflected and delayed, came swiftly once Djabar confessed. Within days of his capture, the Turban Killer was tried and publicly hanged.

DEADLY TRIO

THREE COLOMBIANS ARE RESPONSIBLE FOR A PRODIGIOUS NUMBER OF VICTIMS

Just how does it happen that three of the world's most infamous serial killers have come from Colombia? Collectively, they have confessed to some 500 murders, and their victims include hundreds of children. Seven hundred or more victims may have fallen prey to this South American trio.

THE BEAST

Luis Alfredo Garavito Cubillos of Génova, Colombia, was convicted of raping and murdering 140 victims, and perhaps another 160 should be attributed to him. Born in January 1957, Garavito was primarily active in the 1990s. His crimes earned him the nickname of La Bestia (The Beast).

Garavito's victims, all boys between the ages of 6 and 16, came from very poor families or were living on the streets. Garavito

In Brazil police announced that Thiago Henrique Gomes da Rocha had confessed to murdering 39 people, including 16 young women, over four years. According to police, Rocha shot his victims while riding by on his motorcycle. His female victims bore a strong resemblance to his fiancée, police said.

sometimes pretended to be a cleric or the representative of a charitable organization, ruses that got him invited to speak at schools and gave him easy access to fresh victims. But his specialty was abducting homeless boys who would not be missed if they disappeared. He would lure a victim with money or a small gift and then persuade the youngster to walk with him to an isolated spot, where Garavito sexually abused him and finally slit his throat. The bodies of many of his victims showed signs of prolonged torture.

In April 1999, Garavito's capture brought his reign of terror to an end. But Colombians have not rested easy. At the time of his conviction, neither the death penalty nor life imprisonment were permitted by law. Legislation passed since then allows incarceration for up to 60 years, and the new standard, if applied to Garavito, would almost certainly continue to keep him off the streets—surely the most desirable outcome, since Garavito has expressed the desire to work with abused children upon his release.

THE MONSTER OF THE ANDES

Pedro Alonso López was born in Santa Isabel, Colombia, in the 1940s. At the age of 18, already a survivor of sexual assault, he stole a car and was sent to prison, where he was gang raped. He restored his honor by killing three of his attackers. That act of revenge added time to his sentence, but prison authorities saw the murders as motivated by self-defense, and López was paroled.

He moved to Peru and began preying on young girls, mainly from the country's northern indigenous groups. When members of the Ayacucho tribe caught him trying to kidnap a 9-year-old girl, they seized him with the intention of burying him alive. But an American missionary intervened. She persuaded them to spare the captive's life, and López was handed over to the police, who soon released him.

He returned to Colombia and essentially picked up where he had left off. He traveled widely around the country and into Ecuador as well, feeding his craving for fresh victims and killing them only in the daylight hours so that his pleasure in watching them die would not be diminished by the darkness of night. López particularly enjoyed staring into a little girl's eyes

as he strangled her. He later reported having raped and killed at a rate of three girls a week.

Meanwhile, authorities in both countries thought slavery or prostitution rings must be behind the puzzling disappearance of so many young girls. They had no evidence, no suspects, and no reason to believe anything else until April 1980, when a flash flood near Ambato, Ecuador, suddenly uncovered the bodies of four missing children.

Now the police were on the hunt. López was leading a 12-year-old girl away from an outdoor marketplace when her mother noticed and gave chase. Traders and other townspeople joined the pursuit and held López until the police arrived.

López confessed to the murder of 110 girls in Ecuador, about 100 more in Colombia, and what he claimed were many more than 100 in Peru. Even though he led authorities to the graves of more than 50 of his victims, police in Ecuador found his tale of horror so incredible that it took substantiation from their colleagues in Colombia and Peru for them to accept it, and for López to become known as the Monster of the Andes.

But the story doesn't end there. Thanks to the peculiarities of the

Ecuadorean legal system, a sentence of life in prison normally means serving no more than 16 years, and López was duly released. There have been confusing and contradictory reports of his deportation back to Colombia, his confinement in a psychiatric hospital, and his release from that facility. The upshot is that the Monster of the Andes remains at large, his whereabouts unknown.

THE SAVAGE OF THE MANGROVE SWAMP

Daniel Camargo Barbosa, a Colombian born in 1930, had been convicted of theft by the late 1950s. Although Camargo and his common-law wife had two children, he was involved with another woman he planned to marry. But that plan came to a halt when Camargo discovered that his bride-to-be was not a virgin. To save their relationship, they agreed that she would procure young virgins for him, drug them, and deliver them for defloration. None of these victims were killed, but the crimes were exposed, and the pair went to prison in 1964.

Camargo was released after eight years. In 1974 he committed his first murder. The victim was a 9-year-old schoolgirl. He raped her and then killed her. But he failed to cover his tracks, and he went to prison a second time. This sentence was for 25 years, in a prison on an island.

Camargo managed to escape in 1984. Given the setting, prison authorities assumed he'd either drowned or been eaten

When Daniel Camargo Barbosa was captured, his briefcase contained his last victim's bloody clothes and a paperback copy of Dostoyevsky's *Crime and Punishment*.

UNDER PRESSURE

A form of asphyxia, strangulation is characterized by a lack of oxygen to the brain. Without a continuous supply of oxygen, unconsciousness can occur in just 10 seconds and brain death within four minutes. With just four pounds of pressure applied, the jugular veins can become blocked, while the average handshake involves about 80-100 pounds of pressure.

by sharks. But in fact he went to Ecuador, reached Quito, and began his career as a serial killer.

Between 1984 and 1986 he lured as many as 54 young girls into a mangrove swamp, where he raped and killed them and then dismembered their bodies and left the pieces for carrion birds and other scavengers to eat. Police searching for the missing girls focused their investigation on gangs in the area, not believing that just one person could be responsible for so many disappearances.

Camargo tripped himself up when a missing 9-year-old girl's bloody clothing was found in his possession. He confessed to her murder and to having killed a total of 72 other girls since his 1984 escape from the island prison.

He was convicted of his crimes in 1989. But because he was in Ecuador, he was sentenced to only 16 years, like Pedro Alonso López, who was in the same prison at the time. In 1994, before Camargo could be released, he was killed by another inmate, the cousin of one of his victims.

UNHOLY MOSES

A SERIAL KILLER MARCHES TO PRETORIA

Between 1994 and 1995, Moses Sithole raped and murdered more than 30 women in the South African towns of Atteridgeville, Boksburg, and Cleveland. His terrifying crimes became known as the work of the ABC Killer.

Sithole would pose as the manager of a fake charitable organization, Youth Against Human Abuse. The so-called charity gave him an excuse to conduct "job interviews" with his victims. At the right moment, he would ask the trusting female applicant to walk with him across a field to "headquarters," and once the two of them were out of sight, he would rape her and then strangle her with her underwear. The "interview" often concluded with Sithole scrawling *BITCH* on the victim's body.

In August 1995, Sithold panicked when he was spotted with one of the victims. First he fled, then he called a local journalist, Tamsen de Beer, and told her he was the ABC Killer. De Beer tipped off the police, but they failed to apprehend him. Two months later, he was betrayed by his brother-in-law, arrested, and charged with 38 murders, 40 rapes, and 6 robberies.

Sithole is currently serving a 2,410-year sentence in Pretoria Central Prison.

TALL, HANDSOME, AND DARK

BAD BOY TED BUNDY CONFESSED TO 35 MURDERS

Ted Bundy, suave and charismatic, was well-spoken and had a facile charm. He moved with ease between social and professional roles, from University of Washington psychology major to night-shift volunteer for a suicide-prevention hotline, from clean-cut law student to manager of a presidential candidate's local campaign office, from governor's aide to employee of the Washington State agency that was directing the search for the young women who had been disappearing since the beginning of 1974, sometimes at a rate of two or three a month.

Bundy had a way with young women, and he had his type—white, usually middle class, often a college student, average age 19, though the oldest of his victims was 26 and seven were girls under 18, including one who was 13. His final victim was a 12-year-old girl he lured away from her Florida classroom.

Bundy could always get a young woman to trust him, as long as he didn't break into her apartment or slip uninvited into her

Left: Ted Bundy acting like the madman he was in the courtroom after the judge had departed.

sorority house or descend on her from the shadows of an alley or a parking lot. Women and girls responded to the quiet authority of the detective who introduced himself as Officer Roseland and asked them to come with him. They were happy to lend a hand when the good-looking young man with his arm in a sling, the polite young man with his foot in a cast, or the helpless-looking young man on crutches lost his grip on a stack of books or asked their help in wrestling an unwieldy package into his VW Beetle.

He used their bodies sexually, sometimes washing their hair and making up their faces until time and the elements took their toll.

He loved their bodies. Over and over he returned to where he'd hidden them in Taylor Mountain Forest on the eastern flank of King County in Washington, and in different remote sites outside Seattle—as well as in five other states. He used their bodies sexually, sometimes washing their hair and making up their faces until time and the elements took their toll. He removed several of their heads and kept them with him for as long as they lasted. In Seattle, he cremated one of them in his girlfriend's fireplace.

From the Pacific Northwest to the Florida Panhandle, the recovered body of every victim except one bore Bundy's signatures. Their throats spoke to the power of his hands. Virtually

Theodore Bundy watches intently during the third day of jury selection at his trial in Orlando for the murder of 12-year-old Kimberly Leach.

every staved-in skull told a story of homicidal frenzy. Some of the skulls had a hole where the front teeth had been.

It was a forensic match between a mold of Bundy's own teeth and photographs of bite wounds suffered in January 1978 by one of two murdered sorority sisters in Tallahassee that finally landed Bundy on death row in Florida—that, and the recollection of a school crossing guard in Lake City who reported having seen Bundy just weeks later, in February, as the killer led his 12-year-old victim toward a parked van.

Awaiting trial, Bundy seemed unconcerned. After all, in Colorado in 1977 he had escaped custody twice. In June of that year he jumped from an open courthouse window and was on the loose for six days before being recaptured. At the end of December, he broke out of his prison cell, went to Chicago, and headed south from there.

He was offered a plea deal in the killing of the two sorority women—a fixed sentence of 75 years in exchange for his

THE PORN DEFENSE

On the eve of his execution, Ted Bundy spoke at length with an interviewer about his addiction to violent pornography. In a porn-saturated culture, Bundy claimed, it's not difficult for some people to lose the distinction between sexual attraction and enraged lust, or between consensual sex and rape.

admission of guilt. But he refused. Against his attorneys' advice, he insisted on handling many aspects of his own defense. Bundy was convicted of the two murders, and on July 30, 1979, he was handed two sentences of death. Six months later, Bundy was convicted of abducting and murdering the Lake City schoolgirl, and in February 1980 a third death sentence was imposed for this crime.

The next several years were taken up with a series of appeals, all of which Bundy lost. In 1984, hoping for a stay of execution, he began to confess his earlier unsolved murders in Washington, Oregon, Idaho, Utah, and Colorado, and promised more. The plan worked, twice—in July and again in November of 1986, he obtained a stay shortly before his scheduled execution, once with a margin of seven hours and once with only 15 minutes to spare.

Bundy revived this successful strategy in 1988, when he confessed to still more murders. But there were to be no more stays. Bundy was electrocuted by the State of Florida on the morning of January 24, 1989.

TIMELINE OF TERROR

SOME OF TED BUNDY'S KNOWN AND CONFIRMED MURDERS OF WOMEN AND GIRLS

1974

February 1 21-year-old abducted from the house she shared with roommates in Seattle

March 12 19-year-old abducted from the campus of Evergreen State College, Olympia, Washington

April 17 18-year-old abducted from the campus of Central Washington State University, Ellensburg

May 6 22-year-old abducted from the campus of Oregon State University, Corvallis

June 1 22-year-old last seen leaving the Flame Tavern in Burien, Washington

June 11 18-year-old abducted from behind her sorority house near the University of Washington campus

July 14 23-year-old and 19-year-old taken in separate abductions several hours apart from Lake Sammamish State Park in Issaquah, Washington

October 2 16-year-old abducted from Holladay, Utah

October 18 17-year-old abducted outside a pizza parlor in Midvale, Utah

October 31 17-year-old abducted from a Halloween party in Lehi, Utah

November 8 17-year-old abducted from a school parking lot in Bountiful, Utah

1975

January 12 23-year-old from Michigan abducted from her hotel while on a ski trip with her fiancé in Snowmass, Colorado

March 15 26-year-old abducted near a tavern in Vail, Colorado

April 6 25-year-old abducted while bicycling near Grand Junction, Colorado

May 6 13-year-old abducted from a school playground in Pocatello, Idaho

June 28 15-year-old abducted from the campus of Brigham Young University, Provo, Utah

1978

January 15 20-year-old and 21-year-old murdered at Chi Omega sorority house, Florida State University, Tallahassee

February 9 12-year-old abducted from her junior high school in Lake City, Florida

POGO THE CLOWN'S DARK SIDE

JOHN WAYNE GACY WAS A CLOWN, A CONTRACTOR, AND COLD-BLOODED KILLER

B orn in 1942 and brought up in Chicago, John Wayne Gacy (right) married young. He took on the management of his father-in-law's three Kentucky Fried Chicken franchises in Waterloo, Iowa, and proved adept at the business. Gacy and his wife quickly had two children, a boy and a girl. The couple became respected members of the business community, with Gacy earning a reputation as a tireless volunteer for various clubs.

But Gacy was harboring a big secret about himself, and it burst into the open on May 10, 1968. Much to the shock of his friends and associates, to say nothing of his wife, Gacy was arrested and charged with coercing a 15-year-old male employee into oral sodomy and attempting to sexually assault another boy, aged 16.

Gacy supplied a third youth with mace and paid him $300 to "encourage" the 15-year-old not to testify in court. But the young would-be hatchet man was arrested for assault and confessed the whole plan. In the end, Gacy admitted his guilt

POLICE DEPT.
DES PLAINES, ILL.
78 - 467 · 12-22-78

SERIAL KILLER ART

John Wayne Gacy devoted many hours to oil painting during his 14 years on death row. Among his subjects were clowns, birds, skulls, Jeffrey Dahmer, Elvis Presley, Mickey Mouse, Jesus, John F. Kennedy, Adolph Hitler, Disney's Seven Dwarfs, and a self-portrait entitled "Goodbye Pogos." Gacy gave the paintings to pen pals.

and was sentenced to 10 years in prison. On the day of his sentencing, his wife filed for divorce, and he never saw her or their children again.

In 1971, after serving only 18 months of his 10-year term, Gacy was paroled on condition that he return to Chicago, live with his mother, and observe a 10 p.m. curfew. He got a job as a chef at a Chicago restaurant, and with his mother's assistance he bought a house at 8213 West Summerdale Avenue in Norwood Park Township, outside Chicago. One feature of the house was a crawl space four feet deep, with a dirt floor.

Also in 1971, Gacy had a brush with the law—he was charged with disorderly conduct when a gay youth claimed that Gacy had tried to rape him. But the young man failed to appear in court, and the charges were dismissed. Gacy's parole board never heard about the incident, and shortly afterward his parole came to an end.

A second close call came in June 1972, when another young man told police that Gacy, impersonating a sheriff, had lured him into a vehicle and forced him to perform oral sex. In this case, too, the charges were dropped. By this time, Gacy had committed his first murder, six months

Grid patterns are drawn on the lawn where Chicago police planned to excavate for more possible victims of serial killer John Wayne Gacy.

before. The victim was a young man Gacy had picked up at Chicago's Greyhound bus station.

June 1972 was also the year that Gacy remarried. His second wife, a divorcée, had two daughters. Gacy moved his new family into his house and continued to cruise Chicago's Loop and Near North Side in search of hustlers and runaways.

As before, he lured some of his victims into his car by posing as a law enforcement officer. Others he simply picked up and took back to the house on West Summerdale, if his wife and

Stephen Koschal with the paintings of serial killer John Wayne Gacy he is selling at AAA Antiques Mall. Koschal is holding Gacy's self portrait, titled "Pogo the Clown."

stepdaughters happened to be away. There he used handcuffs to perform "magic tricks" that left his victims helpless to resist sexual abuse and garroting. In fact, Gacy's "rope trick" became one of his signatures—he would strangle his victim to death and then conceal the body in the crawl space under his house.

In 1975 Gacy launched his career as a construction contractor. In 1976 his second marriage ended. Newly single, he was free to turn his home into a slaughterhouse. He was also building a reputation as a successful entrepreneur. Over the next two years, in addition to running his business, he got involved in Democratic Party politics, and in time became a party precinct captain. He also began performing for children as Pogo the Clown. Gacy appeared in character at several Democratic Party fundraisers, and in May 1978 he was photographed with First Lady Rosalynn Carter.

By this time, the bodies were piling up. There were already 27 in the crawl space. When neighbors asked Gacy about the foul odors wafting from his property, he waved their questions away with vague explanations involving a faulty sewer line.

But the more serious problem for Gacy was that he was running out of room. He had already retrofitted the crawl space with drainage trenches, and from time to time he poured quicklime over the bodies, to accelerate their decomposition and get them to the point where he could cover the whole collection with a camouflaging layer of cement. He considered enlarging the crawl space. He gave some thought to warehousing fresh bodies in the attic. In the meantime, he improvised by burying two bodies outside the house. But then

DID YOU KNOW

On May 22, 1978 John Wayne Gacy kidnapped and chloroformed Jeffrey Rignall, 26. Gacy strapped Rignall to a torture rack, raped him for days with an assortment of phallic prostheses, and dumped what he thought was Rignall's dead body in Lincoln Park (shown below). But Rignall survived and told police the details of the attack.

it occurred to him that there was no reason not to begin hurling bodies from one of the two bridges over the Des Plaines River on Interstate 55. And in 1978, with his crawl space at capacity, that's exactly how Gacy disposed of his last four victims.

On December 22 of that year, police armed with a warrant went to Gacy's house in search of Robert Piest, 15, missing since December 11 and last seen with Gacy outside the pharmacy where the boy worked. The officers immediately identified the stench of rotting flesh and organized a search of the property.

In March 1980, John Wayne Gacy was convicted of murdering 33 boys and young men between 1972 and 1978. He spent 14 years on death row, a period during which he took up oil painting. He was put to death by lethal injection at the Stateville Penitentiary in Joliet, Illinois, on May 10, 1994—26 years to the day from his first arrest for sexual assault of an adolescent boy.

SHEDDING A TOXIC SHAME

A DAUGHTER'S JOURNEY BEYOND HER FATHER'S CRIMES

Keith Hunter Jesperson (above), a long-haul trucker, killed eight women in the Pacific Northwest between 1990 and 1995. After raping and strangling one of his victims, he strapped her body facedown to the underside of his truck so the vehicle's motion would obliterate her face and fingerprints.

While he was killing, Jesperson wrote many detailed anonymous confessions signed with the happy face icon, and mailed them to prosecutors and media figures. Phil Stanford, then a columnist for *The Oregonian*, wrote several pieces about Jesperson and dubbed him the Happy Face Killer.

When Jesperson was finally arrested, his estranged daughter was 15 years old. Melissa Jesperson had been separated from her father five years before, when her parents divorced, but she had many fond memories of him. And yet there were also memories she couldn't put out of her mind, such as the sight of her father hanging a litter of kittens on a clothesline and then breaking their tiny necks.

She found it impossible to free herself from the shame.

Melissa got married at 21. As Melissa Moore, she left her father and his name behind, and soon became a mother. But she found it impossible to free herself from the shame of Jesperson's crimes, and most of all from her fear that she or her two daughters might have inherited his violent proclivities. In time she learned that DNA doesn't work that way. All the same, she kept the identity of her father a secret that she confided only to her husband and to the journals she had been keeping since the time of her father's arrest.

In 2008 Melissa's five-year-old daughter began asking questions about her grandfather. Melissa decided to email Dr. Phil McGraw for help, and several months later she appeared on *Dr. Phil's Get Real Retreat*. From that experience she gained the courage and emotional support to stop bearing the weight of guilt that belonged to her father. Melissa Moore's book, *Shattered Silence: The Untold Story of a Serial Killer's Daughter* is based on her journals and was published in 2009.

Left: Melissa Moore, daughter of Keith Hunter Jesperson, as featured in LMN's TV series *Monster in My Family*.

THE TOP 10

HYBRISTOPHILIACS
A person, often a woman, who is romantically obsessed with violent criminals

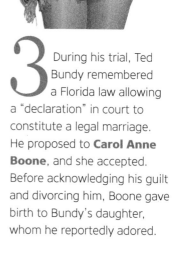

1 The screensaver on **Victoria Redstall's** (pictured right) phone is a picture of Wayne Adam Ford that she took during his trial for murdering and dismembering several prostitutes.

2 A stretch? Fair enough. But **Joyce Carol Oates** did base a famous short story ("Where Are You Going, Where Have You Been?") on Charles Schmid, a killer of teenage girls.

3 During his trial, Ted Bundy remembered a Florida law allowing a "declaration" in court to constitute a legal marriage. He proposed to **Carol Anne Boone**, and she accepted. Before acknowledging his guilt and divorcing him, Boone gave birth to Bundy's daughter, whom he reportedly adored.

4 An attorney and mother of four, **Rosalie Martinez** (pictured below) left her husband for Oscar Ray Bolin Jr., a convicted rapist and murderer she married over the phone.

5 Kenneth Bianchi, half of the Hillside Strangler team, had a good thing going with **Veronica Compton** until she dumped him for Douglas Clark, another serial killer.

6 The true-crime writer **Sondra London** (pictured below) has been romantically involved with three serial killers: Gerald John Schaefer, Keith Jesperson (the Happy Face Killer), and Danny Rolling (the Gainesville Ripper).

7 **Phyllis Wilcox** believed Henry Lee Lucas when he swore he'd never killed anyone but his mother. Hoping to stop Lucas's execution, Wilcox impersonated one of his victims.

8 Every day, bouquet of sweet peas in hand, **Rosalind Bowers**, though married,attended the trial of handsome William Durrant, a killer in late-nineteenth-century San Francisco.

9 As a juror at his trial, **Cindy Haden** fell for Richard Ramirez, the Night Stalker. She felt terrible about voting to convict him of his crimes.

10 At age 18, **Jason Moss** wrote to and met with John Wayne Gacy. Moss lived long enough to tell the tale, but later committed suicide.

CRIME DOES NOT PAY!!!

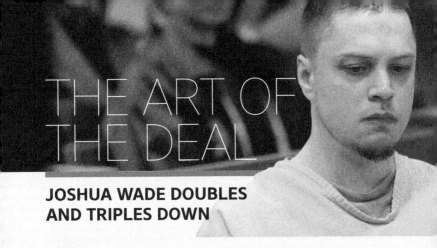

THE ART OF THE DEAL

JOSHUA WADE DOUBLES AND TRIPLES DOWN

Although Joshua Wade was acquitted of murdering Della Brown in 2003, he went to prison for evidence tampering in the case. He served several years behind bars.

Months after his release, Wade was indicted for the kidnapping and murder of Mindy Schloss. As he had done during his first trial, he pleaded not guilty. But, facing federal charges that carried an automatic death penalty, in February 2010 he made a deal with prosecutors: life in prison, in exchange for a guilty plea in Schloss's death and his admission of guilt in Brown's murder.

Constitutional protections against double jeopardy made it impossible for prosecutors to retry Wade for Brown's death. But that previous murder guaranteed so much prison time that Wade would never be released.

Four years later, in 2014, Wade was still wheeling and dealing. This time he wanted to be transferred to a different prison, and agreed to provide information about three more of his killings—one committed when he was 14, another during a robbery that went wrong five years later, and the beating and shooting of the man who was with Brown the night Wade killed her.

Joshua Wade maintains that he is not a serial killer.

WHERE THE TRAIL GOES COLD

CHILLING CRIMES AND
KILLERS ON THE LOOSE

Serial killers do get caught, as we know. But a skillful serial killer can often pass as a normal, well-regarded member of the community and operate for a very long time—or even disappear without ever being captured. As Mark Antony famously says in Shakespeare's *Julius Caesar*, "The evil that men do lives after them."

KARACHI, PAKISTAN

Karachi, the capital of Pakistan's Sindh Province, was already no stranger to violent crime in 2012, when 10 children vanished from several of the city's suburbs. Most of their bodies were recovered, and the victims were found to have been raped, tortured, and strangled.

Several more children disappeared in 2013. The bodies that were found showed the same signs of rape, torture, and strangulation. The evidence pointed to a killer who had acted in a frenzy—many of the victims had severe neck wounds, and vital organs were gouged from their bodies.

By the middle of 2013, the number of vanished children had reached almost 200. The great majority of them remain

THE RAINBOW MANIAC

From February 2007 to August 2008, 13 gay men were murdered in Paturis Park in São Paulo, Brazil. All the victims were between the ages of 20 and 40, and all but one were shot. Police dubbed the killer the Rainbow Maniac, in a reference to the gay pride flag. Officials from the São Paulo State Public Safety Department said they thought the killer might be a state police officer.

missing and unaccounted for. Police in the city have no clues to the children's fate, or to the identity of their presumed killer.

KIGALI, RWANDA

No one knows who was killing women in Kigali between June and September 2012 or why the women were strangled. But at least 15 women, mostly prostitutes, met the same fate during that three-month period. Many had their eyes gouged out. One had the words "I will stop once I have killed 400 prostitutes" carved into her abdomen.

As rumors flew, police dismissed the suggestion that the killings were the work of a deranged patron seeking revenge for contracting HIV. Disagreement over payment for the women's services would have been equally plausible as a motive, police said.

Witnesses reported seeing a pair of men enter two of the women's homes in broad daylight, and the women's bodies were later found inside. The Rwanda National Police arrested two suspects in September, but the investigation continues, as does the community's state of terror over the crimes of what some have called an African Jack the Ripper.

CAPE TOWN AND JOHANNESBURG, SOUTH AFRICA

Between April 2010 and April 2013, nine gay men in and around Cape Town were murdered by one or more killers. The murderers apparently began communicating with the men online before meeting them in person.

By the time of the ninth murder, four of the victims were known to have been killed by the same person, who remained at large. Meanwhile, in Johannesburg, three men had been arrested in what may have been related or copycat killings. Despite the arrests, however, the murders continued. Investigators now suspect that a network of killers may have been involved.

CIUDAD JUÁREZ AND MEXICALI, MEXICO

Ciudad Juárez, just south of El Paso, Texas, may be one of the most dangerous cities in the world. Not only is it a well-known base of operations for drug barons, it also has a reputation for absolutely barbaric crimes against women. Records suggest that since 1993, more than 500 women in Ciudad Juárez have died in attacks by vicious killers. In many of these cases, the killers were arrested and prosecuted, and almost all the murderers have been gang members. At the same time, nearly a third of the women in Ciudad Juárez have been killed in remarkably similar circumstances. And, since 2008, much the same thing has been happening in Mexicali, a city in the far north of Baja California.

Because so many murders in Mexico are related to organized crime, Mexican authorities have generally been slow to consider the possibility that a serial killer might be at work. But that attitude began to shift in July 2011, after the attorney general confirmed that a series of murders in Mexicali were the work not of gangs but of individuals, maybe even a single family. Only two of the murdered women in Mexicali were not prostitutes or drug addicts; their remains were dumped in deserted areas, and some of the bodies were dismembered.

Police in Ciudad Juárez are also seeking an individual serial killer, known locally as the Juárez Predator. But no serial killer has been found to date, and women continue to disappear.

LONG ISLAND, NEW YORK

In recent years, dismembered bodies have been turning up in several remote beach towns on Long Island, east of New York City. The Long Island Killer, as the murderer is called, typically dumps victims near roadways and leaves them unburied in thick vegetation. The killer's techniques have been evolving over time, too, and not all the bodies are now dismembered.

FBI officials believe the attacks are always premeditated. The murderer is someone who obviously knows the shoreline well. Some have suggested that Joel Rifkin, a convicted serial killer, is responsible for at least some of the earliest of these murders. But those suspicions have never been confirmed, and the killings continued even after Rifkin was imprisoned for a series of murders in New York.

EDGECOMBE COUNTY, NORTH CAROLINA

Since 2005, 10 black women and a cross-dressing man have disappeared in Edgecombe County, North Carolina. Nine of these missing persons were later discovered to have been murdered. Edgecombe County residents believe lives

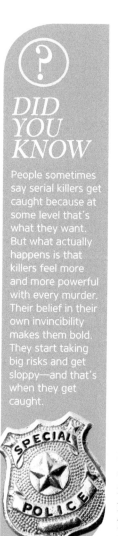

DID YOU KNOW

People sometimes say serial killers get caught because at some level that's what they want. But what actually happens is that killers feel more and more powerful with every murder. Their belief in their own invincibility makes them bold. They start taking big risks and get sloppy—and that's when they get caught.

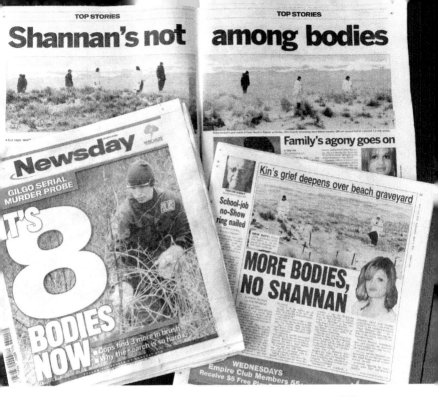

Articles about the recent discovery of bodies found near the town of Gilgo Beach on Long Island, New York. Eight bodies were discovered in the area.

could have been saved if the police had acted sooner, and that the police have done too little too late to solve the murders.

The man and all the women, substance abusers working in the sex trade, are said to have fallen victim to the so-called Seven Bridges Killer, who is almost certainly still at large. Antwan Maurice Pittman was convicted of one of these murders in 2011, and some people suspect that Pittman is the Seven Bridges Killer. But most believe the killer is someone else, since another murder in the same pattern occurred in 2012.

FROM THE MINDS OF BABES

774987 BELL. M.
18-7-77

A GLANCE AT THE WORLD'S YOUNGEST SERIAL KILLERS

MARY BELL AGE: 10-11, 1968
Newcastle-Upon-Tyne, Great Britain
VICTIMS: Two boys, 3 and 4 years of age
METHOD: Strangulation
NOTORIETY: The case made international headlines because of the age of both the criminal and the victims, and Mary (pictured above) was dubbed "The British Bad Seed" after the horror movie *The Bad Seed*. Released from incarceration, she is now a grandmother living under a new identity.

CRAIG PRICE AGE: 13-15, 1987-1989
Warwick, RI, USA
VICTIMS: One adult woman and a second
woman with her 8- and 10-year-old daughters
METHOD: Stabbing and bludgeoning
NOTORIETY: "The Warwick Slasher" reportedly
showed no remorse when arrested; the familial
trio of victims was murdered two years
after his first.

GEORGE STINNEY AGE: 14, 1944
Alcolu, SC, USA
VICTIMS: Two girls, 8 and 11 years of age
METHOD: Bludgeoning
NOTORIETY: The youngest person ever
executed in the United States in the twentieth
century; 70 years later his conviction
was overturned.

ANDREW GOLDEN AGE: 11, AND
MITCHELL JOHNSON AGE: 13, 1998
Warwick, RI, USA
VICTIMS: One teacher and four students
METHOD: Stabbing and bludgeoning
NOTORIETY: Mass murderers rather than
typical serial killers, Golden and his
accomplice Mitchell Johnson are nonetheless
the youngest perpetrators of multiple killings
in recent US history.

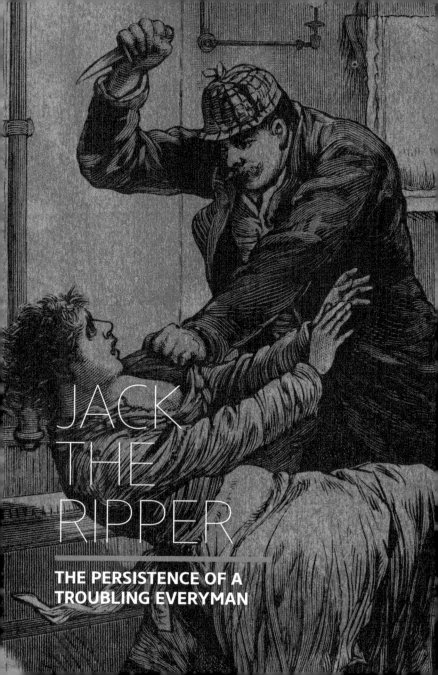

JACK THE RIPPER

THE PERSISTENCE OF A TROUBLING EVERYMAN

More than a century after the serial killer called Jack the Ripper made his presence known in London's Whitechapel neighborhood, his infamy lives on, and so does the public's fascination with him.

Five known murders have been credited to him, but murder in the street was not uncommon in late-nineteenth-century London. Jack the Ripper's notoriety rests on something other than quantity. Certainly, the ferocity of his crimes was something new to the British public of the day. But part of the explanation certainly has to do with the sensational way in which these five murders were reported in the London newspapers of the time. No one disputes that the killings and the killer were real, but some historians believe the figure of Jack the Ripper was largely the invention of newspaper publishers eager to turn a profit by keeping his crimes in the public eye. Even the killer's nickname was a journalistic fabrication.

Another aspect of Jack the Ripper's enduring legend is the fact that he was never captured and remains unidentified. In his own era, and later on as well, the question of who Jack was has invited sober detective work as well as wild speculation, with armchair detectives proposing such unlikely suspects as Britain's Prince Albert and a number of less imposing aristocrats, along with the writer Lewis Carroll.

All Jack the Ripper left behind was the evidence of his crimes, scrutinized only in the limited way the police of his day were capable of But because Jack is both notorious and unknown, he has become a sinister Everyman, an unsettling type of public properly. As such, Jack the Ripper is a magnet for collective imaginings, judgments, and emotions that probably have less to say about a long-dead nineteenth-century serial killer than about the shadowy impulses and fears of the ordinary people of his day, and maybe of our own.

STAR POWER

IT PAYS TO HAVE CONNECTIONS

Sometime in 1977, Kenneth Bianchi and Angelo Buono, cousins and hedonistic killers jointly known as the Hillside Strangler, gave a young woman named Catharine what they intended to be her last ride. When she mentioned that her father was the movie actor Peter Lorre, Bianchi and Buono, great fans of Lorre's work, decided to release the star's daughter unharmed. Only much later, after the killers were arrested and their photographs were made public, did Catharine Lorre realize how close she had come to being murdered. Ironically, one of her father's most memorable roles was that of Hans Beckert, the baby-faced serial killer in Fritz Lang's 1931 film M.

Right: Angelo Buono talks to a woman in front of his upholstery shop as a press conference was being held in Los Angeles announcing that Bianchi would be charged with the murder of 10 of the 13 "Hillside Strangler" victims.

STREET SMARTS
SAVE YOUR LIFE

1 You're approached by a stranger whose body language and friendly words feel out of sync. Don't engage—walk away. You don't owe this person your time or attention.

2 A stranger offers you help you didn't ask for and insists on teaming up with you on some task. Refuse the offer clearly and firmly, and immediately put some distance between the two of you. Run, if necessary, and don't hesitate to call for help if the situation escalates.

3 An apparently weak or disabled stranger asks you for assistance that requires physical contact. Don't approach. Offer to call for help.

4 A stranger on the street seeks your help with some situation and gives you an elaborate explanation that includes far more information than you need. Too much detail is the classic sign of a confidence game, if not something worse. Walk away.

5 You're driving on a lightly traveled road or isolated stretch of highway, and you see a stranded motorist up ahead. Don't stop to help. Call the police and report a driver with car trouble at that spot.

A PARTING
THOUGHT

"It wasn't as dark and scary as it sounds. I had a lot of fun . . . killing somebody's a funny experience."
—ALBERT DESALVO

SOURCES

Aamodt, M. G. (2014, September 6). Serial killer statistics. Accessed June 28, 2015. http://maamodt.asp.radford.edu/serial killer information center/ project description.htm

Amicus Curiae (blog). "A Murderous Phenomenon: Female Serial Killers." March 15, 2011. sites.law.lsu.edu/amicus-curiae/2011/03/15/ a-murderous-phenomenon-female-serial-killers.

Anthes, Emily. "Lady Killers." The New Yorker. Accessed June 28, 2015. http:// www.newyorker.com/tech/elements/female-serial-killers

Associated Press. "Alaska Serial Killer Wants to Trade Authorities Info on Three Unknown Victims in Exchange for a Prison Transfer." Daily Mail. June 20, 2014. www.dailymail.co.uk/news/article-2663989/ Alaska-serial-killer-wants-trade-authorities-info-three-unknown-victims-exchange-prison-transfer.html.

Associated Press. "Sale of Chicago Serial Killer's Art Draws Protests: A Florida Collector Says He Sees Nothing Wrong with Selling the Works by John Wayne Gacy." St. Petersburg Times. June 6, 2004. www.sptimes. com/2004/06/06/State/Sale_of_Chicago_seria.shtml.

BBC News. "Colombian Child Killer Confesses." October 30, 1999. news.bbc.co.uk/2/hi/americas/493887.stm.

Bio. "Infamous Serial Killers." Accessed May 18, 2015. www.biography.com/people/groups/serial-killers.

Bonn, Scott. "5 Myths about Serial Killers and Why They Persist." Scientific American. October 24, 2014. http://www.scientificamerican.com/ article/5-myths-about-serial-killers-and-why-they-persist-excerpt/.

Bovsun, Mara. "Pied Piper of Tucson: Twisted 1960s Killings by Charles Howard Schmid, Jr." New York Daily News. December 19, 2009. www.nydailynews.com/news/crime/pied-piper-tucson-twisted-1960s-killings-charles-howard-schmid-jr-article-1.434271.

Bowden, Charles. Murder City: Ciudad Juárez and the Global Economy's New Killing Fields. New York: Nation Books, 2010.

Broomfield, Nick, and Joan Churchill. Aileen: Life and Death of a Serial Killer. DVD. Thousand Oaks, CA: First Look Studios, 2003.

Capital News. "Wave of Prostitute Murders Stokes Fear in Rwanda." September 1, 2012. www.capitalfm.co.ke/news/2012/09/ wave-of-prostitute-murders-stokes-fear-in-rwanda.

Castle, T., and C Hensley. "Serial Killers with Military Experience: Applying Learning Theory to Serial Murder." International Journal of Offender Therapy and Comparative Criminology 46 (August 2002): 453–65.

Cleckley, Hervey M. *The Mask of Sanity: An Attempt to Clarify Some Issues About the So-Called Psychopathic Personality*. Facsimile reprint, 1950 edition. Eastford, CT: Martino Fine Books, 2015.

CrimeZZZ.net. "Serial Killer Crime Index." Accessed May 18, 2015. www.crimezzz.net/index.php.

Criminal Justice USA. "10 Infamous Female Serial Killers." April 7, 2011. www.criminaljusticeusa.com/blog/2011/10-infamous-female-serial-killers.

Davies, Emily. "My Dad Was a Serial Killer . . . and I Worried I Would Turn Out Like Him." DailyMail. April 1, 2013. www.dailymail.co.uk/news/article-2302404/Melissa-Moore-daughter-Happy-Face-serial-killer-Keith-Jesperson-I-worried-I-turn-like-him.html.

Davis, Donald A. *The Jeffrey Dahmer Story: An American Nightmare*. New York: St. Martin's Press, 1991.

Dekle, George R. Sr. *The Last Murder: The Investigation, Prosecution, and Execution of Ted Bundy*. Santa Barbara, CA: Praeger, 2011.

Derrida, Jacques. "Force of Law: The 'Mystical Foundation of Authority.'" Translated by Mary Quaintance. In Drucilla Cornell, Michel Rosenfeld, and David Gray Carlson, eds., *Deconstruction and the Possibility of Justice*. New York: Routledge, 1992: 3–67.

Dodd, Vikram. "Joanne Dennehy Given Whole-Life Jail Sentence for Triple Murder." *The Guardian*. February 28, 2014. www.theguardian.com/uk-news/2014/feb/28/joanna-dennehy-whole-life-jail-sentence.

Epstein, Su C. "The New Mythic Monster." In Jeff Ferrell and Clinton R. Sanders, eds., *Cultural Criminology*. Boston: Northeastern University Press, 1995, 66–79.

Evil Ladies: The World's Most Evil Women. Accessed May 18, 2015. www.evilladies.com.

Ferguson, George, Emily Downing, Kaylor Eutsler, and David Disque. *Paul Durousseau: The Jacksonville Serial Killer*. Radford, VA: Department of Psychology, Radford University, 2006. Accessed May 18, 2015. maamodt.asp.radford.edu/Psyc%20405/serial%20killers/Durousseau,%20Paul%20_Fall,%202006_.pdf.

Fox, James Alan, and Jack Levin. *Extreme Killing: Understanding Serial and Mass Murder*, 2nd ed. Thousand Oaks, CA: Sage, 2012.

Giannangelo, Stephen J. *Real-Life Monsters: A Psychological Examination of the Serial Murderer*. Santa Barbara, CA: Praeger, 2012.

Godwin, G. Maurice. *Hunting Serial Predators*. Sudbury, MA: Jones and Bartlett, 2008.

Greig, Charlotte. *Evil Serial Killers: In the Minds of Monsters*. London: Arcturus Publishing, 2006.

Haggerty, Kevin D. "Modern Serial Killers." *Crime Media Culture: An International Journal* 5 (2009): 168–87.

Harrison, Marissa. "Female serial killers have some shocking characteristics." Business Insider. Accessed July 1, 2015. http://www.businessinsider.com/how-do-female-psychopaths-differ-from-male-psychopaths-2015-6

Haugen, Brenda. *The Zodiac Killer: Terror and Mystery*. Mankato, MN: Compass Point Books, 2011.

Hickey, Eric W. *Serial Murderers and Their Victims*. 6th ed. Belmont, CA: Wadsworth, 2013.

History.com. "This Day in History: Black Magic, Voodoo, and Murder Occurs at Rancho Santa Elena." March 13, 1989. history.com/this-day-in-history/black-magic-voodoo-and-murder-occurs-at-rancho-santa-elena.

Holland, Megan. "Wade Confesses to Two Murders in Plea Deal." *Alaska Dispatch News*. February 6, 2010. www.adn.com/article/20100216/wade-confesses-two-murders-plea-deal.

Holmes, Ronald M., and Stephen T. Holmes. *Serial Murder*. 3rd ed. Thousand Oaks, CA: Sage, 2010.

Holmes, Stephen T., Richard Tewksbury, and Ronald M. Holmes. "Fractured Identity Syndrome: A New Theory of Serial Murder." *Journal of Contemporary Criminal Justice* 15 (1999): 262–72.

Jenkins, John Philip. "Ted Bundy: American Serial Killer." *Encyclopaedia Britannica*. Accessed May 18, 2015. britannica.com/EBchecked/topic/853405/Ted-Bundy.

Johnston, Joni E. "Female Serial Killers: Silent But Deadly." Psychology Today. May 29, 2012. www.psychologytoday.com/blog/the-human-equation/201205/female-serial-killers.

Jones, Richard. "Welcome to Jack the Ripper 1888." Jack the Ripper 1888: The Whitechapel Murders History Resource. Accessed May 18, 2015. www.jack-the-ripper.org.

Kelleher, Michael D., and C. I. Kelleher. *Murder Most Rare: The Female Serial Killer*. New York: Dell, 1999.

Keppel, Robert D., and Stephen Michaud. *Terrible Secrets: Ted Bundy on Serial Murder*. University Place, WA: Mt. 7 Productions, 2012.

Kotz, Pete. "Antwan Maurice Pittman: Have Police Caught a Serial Killer in Rocky Mount, North Carolina?" True Crime Report. September 2, 2009. www.truecrimereport.com/2009/09/antwan_maurice_pittman_have_po.php.

Kristof, Nicholas. "When the Rapist Doesn't See It as Rape." *New York Times*. May 23, 2015. www.nytimes.com/2015/05/24/opinion/sunday/nicholas-kristof-when-the-rapist-doesnt-see-it-as-rape.html.

Larsen, Erik. *The Devil in the White City: Murder, Magic, and Madness at the Fair That Changed America*. New York: Crown, 2003.

Linedecker, Clifford. *Thrill Killers*. Toronto: Paper Jacks, 1988.

MacDonald, John M. "The Threat to Kill." *American Journal of Psychiatry* 120 (1963): 125–30.

Mezzofiore, Gianluca. "'African Jack the Ripper' Kills 15 Prostitutes in Rwanda." *International Business Times*. September 7, 2012. www.ibtimes.co.uk/rwanda-jack-ripper-africa-kigali-prostitute-381895.

Moore, Melissa. "My Evil Dad: Life as a Serial Killer's Daughter." BBC News. November 3, 2014. www.bbc.com/news/magazine-29835159.

Moore, Melissa G., with M. Bridget Cook. *Shattered Silence: The Untold Story of a Serial Killer's Daughter*. Springville, UT: CFI, 2009.

Morton, Robert J., and Mark A. Hilts. *Serial Murder: Multi-Disciplinary Perspectives for Investigators*. Quantico, VA: Federal Bureau of Investigation, 2008.

Morton, Robert J., Jennifer M. Tillman, and Stephanie J. Gaines. *Serial Murder: Pathways for Investigations*. Quantico, VA: Federal Bureau of Investigation, 2014.

Moss, Jason, with Jeffrey Kottler. *The Last Victim: A True-Life Journey into the Mind of the Serial Killer*. New York: Grand Central, 1999.

Murderpedia: The Encyclopedia of Murderers. Accessed May 18, 2015. http://murderpedia.org.

News.com. "Alleged Serial Killer Tiago Henrique Gomes da Rocha: Murders 'Relieved My Anxiety.'" October 19, 2014. www.news.com.au/world/alleged-serial-killer-tiago-henrique-gomes-da-rocha-murders-relieved-my-anxiety/story-fndir2ev-1227095032953.

Newton, Michael. *The Encyclopedia of Serial Killers*. 2nd ed. New York: Facts On File, 2006.

New York Times. "Mrs. Gunness Was Money Mad." May 7, 1908.

Norris, Joel. *Serial Killers: The Growing Menace*. New York: Doubleday, 1988.

Oates, Joyce Carol. *Where Are You Going, Where Have You Been? Selected Early Stories*. Princeton, NJ: Ontario Review Press, 1994.

@onionSlayer. "Serial Killers by Country (List and Map)." Accessed May 17, 2015. www.targetmap.com/viewer.aspx?reportId=6860.

Pearson, Patricia. *When She Was Bad: Violent Women and the Myth of Innocence*. New York: Viking, 1997.

Radford University/Florida Gulf Coast University. "Serial Killer Database."

Last updated September 6, 2014. maamodt.asp.radford.edu/Serial%20 Killer%20Information%20Center/Serial%20Killer%20Statistics.pdf.

Roghay, Sidrah. "Karachi: A Town Where Parents Think Twice before Sending Kids Out." *News International*. April 21, 2013. www.thenews.com.pk/ Todays-News-4-172555-A-town-where-parents-think-twice-before-sending-kids-out.

Rowlands, Ted. "I Am Charles Manson's Wife." CNN.com. November 17, 2014. www.cnn.com/2014/08/09/justice/charles-manson-wife/index.html.

Schmid, David. *Natural Born Celebrities: Serial Killers in American Culture*. Chicago: University of Chicago Press, 2005.

Schram, Pamela J., and Stephen G. Tibbetts. *Introduction to Criminology: Why Do They Do It?* Thousand Oaks, CA: Sage, 2013.

Simpson, Sammie. "10 Serial Killers with Obsessive Groupies." TheRichest.com. June 21, 2014. www.therichest.com/rich-list/most-shocking/ fatal-attraction-10-serial-killers-with-obsessive-groupies/?view=all.

Strand, Ginger. *Killer on the Road: Violence and the American Interstate*. Austin, TX: University of Texas Press, 2012.

Strauss, Eric M., and Jessica Haddad. "Daughter of the 'Happy Face Killer' Talks About Growing Up with a Serial Killer Dad." ABC News. August 20, 2010. abcnews.go.com/2020/daughter-serial-killer-tells-happy-face-killer/story?id=11413812.

Sullivan, Terry, with Peter T. Maiken. *Killer Clown*. New York: Grosset & Dunlap, 1983.

Tanay, Emanuel. "Ted Bundy's 'Suicide.'" Dr. Tanay's Blog. February 28, 2013. drtanay.wordpress.com/2013/02/28/ted-bundys-suicide.

Thornton, Janey Street. "Ninth Gay Man Killed in Suspected Serial Murders in South Africa." *Gay Star News*. April 18, 2013. www.gaystarnews.com/article/ ninth-gay-man-killed-suspected-serial-murders-south-africa180413.

Tuckman, Jo. "Little Old Lady Killer Handed 759 Years in a Mexican Prison." *The Guardian*. April 2, 2008. www.theguardian.com/world/2008/apr/02/ mexico.

Vann, Sonya C. "Owner Will Turn Gacy's Art to Ashes." *Chicago Tribune*. May 18, 1994. articles.chicagotribune.com/1994-05-18/news/9405180294_1_john-wayne-gacy-paintings-joseph-roth.

Vronsky, Peter. *Serial Killers: The Method and Madness of Monsters*. New York: Berkley Books, 2004.

"Worldwide hangings." True Crime Library. Accessed June 30, 2015. http://www. truecrimelibrary.com/crime_series_show.php?id=686&series_number=13

INDEX

CONTINUE THE
CONVERSATION

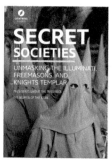
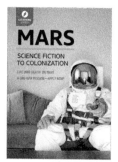

CPSIA information can be obtained at www.ICGtesting.com
Printed in the USA
BVOW11s1516061015

420834BV00003B/3/P

9 781942 411338